Contents

Longer Sukhavati
- Vyuha Sutra

Amitayurdhyana Sutra

Shorter Sukh. Sutra

The Infinite Life Sutra
as Expounded by the Buddha

Translated into Chinese during the Cao-Wei Dynasty
by Tripiṭaka Master Saṃghavarman of India

Part One

Thus have I heard. At one time the Buddha was residing on Vulture Peak, at the citadel of Rājagṛha. An assembly of great monks of twelve thousand members attended, all of whom were great sages who had mastered the spiritual powers. Their names were the Venerable Ājñātakauṇḍinya, the Venerable Aśvajit, the Venerable Bāṣpa, the Venerable Mahānāman, the Venerable Bhadrajit, the Venerable Vimala, the Venerable Yaśodeva, the Venerable Subāhu, the Venerable Pūrṇa, the Venerable Gavāṃpati, the Venerable Uruvilvākāśyapa, the Venerable Gayākāśyapa, the Venerable Nadīkāśyapa, the Venerable Mahākāśyapa, the Venerable Śāriputra, the Venerable Mahāmaudgalyāyana, the Venerable Kapphina, the Venerable Mahākauṣṭhilya, the Venerable Mahākātyāyana, the Venerable Mahācunda, the Venerable Pūrṇamaitrāyaṇīputra, the Venerable Aniruddha, the Venerable Revata, the Venerable Kimpila, the Venerable Amogharāja, the Venerable Pārāyaṇika, the Venerable Vakkula, the Venerable Nanda, the Venerable Svāgata, the Venerable Rāhula, and the Venerable Ānanda. All were equally elders like this.

Bodhisattvas of Mahayana Buddhism also attended the assembly, including all the bodhisattvas of this auspicious cosmic age such as Samantabhadra, Mañjuśrī, and Maitreya. In addition, there were Bhadrapāla and the rest of the group of sixteen bodhisattvas, along with Good Reflection Bodhisattva, Faith Wisdom Bodhisattva, Emptiness Void Bodhisattva, Divine Power Blossom Bodhisattva, Glowing Laurels Bodhisattva, Wisdom Supreme Bodhisattva, Knowledge Banner Bodhisattva, Quiescent Root Bodhisattva, Invoking Wisdom Bodhisattva, Musky Elephant Bodhisattva, Jewel Laurels Bodhisattva, Center Dwelling Bodhisattva, Restrained Conduct Bodhisattva, Emancipation Bodhisattva among others.

All of them, following the model of virtue set by Samanta-bhadra, are endowed with the immeasurable practices and vows of the bodhisattva, and dwell securely in all the virtue and merit of the dharma. They traverse throughout the ten directions, practicing expedient means, enter the storehouse of the dharma of the buddhas, and reach ultimate transcendence, at which, they manifest their supreme perfect enlightenment in immeasurable realms.

Each bodhisattva first dwells in the Tuṣita Heaven where they proclaim the true dharma and then relinquish this heavenly palace to send down their spirit to the womb of a woman.

Born from under the right arm, the bodhisattva takes seven steps in revelation, at which a radiant light shines forth universally illuminating the ten directions and immeasurable buddha lands shake in six ways. Then the bodhisattva proclaims aloud, "I will become the most exalted in this world." Indra and Brahma attend the bodhisattva while celestials and mortals come to pay homage.

The bodhisattva displays mastery of mathematics, literature, archery, and the equestrian arts, expertise in the arts of the sages, and proficiency in classical texts. The bodhisattva enjoys the back garden by training in the martial arts and testing his prowess, and exhibits conjugal life in the palace.

Seeing the old, the sick, and the dead, the bodhisattva realizes the impermanence of the mundane world and renounces kingdom, wealth, and throne to enter the mountains and study the path. The bodhisattva instructs the return of the horse the bodhisattva had ridden and the crown and jewels the bodhisattva had possessed. The bodhisattva discards magnificent apparel to don the garb of an ascetic, shaves head and face of hair, sits upright below a tree, and suffers hardship for six years in ascetic practice as befitting. Having become manifest in this world of the five corruptions, the bodhisattva appears sullied in line with other living beings and cleanses by bathing in a golden stream. A celestial deity bends down a tree branch so that the bodhisattva may climb up from the pool and divine birds flock together to escort the bodhisattva to the seat of awakening.

A youth named Good Fortune appears having perceived the portent of enlightenment, and from him the bodhisattva gratefully receives the gift of rushes, spreads them below the bodhi tree and sits there in a cross-legged position. The bodhisattva emits a great radiant light, by which Māra is alerted. Māra leading his hordes arrives to test the bodhisattva with temptations, but they are controlled through the power of the bodhisattva's wisdom and are all subjugated.

The bodhisattva attains the sublime dharma and realizes supreme perfect enlightenment, and then is approached by Indra and Brahma and asked to turn the wheel of the dharma. At which, the bodhisattva journeys roaring the lion's roar of a buddha, beating the drum of the dharma, trumpeting the horn of the dharma, brandishing the sword of the dharma, raising the banner of the dharma, rolling the thunder of the dharma, striking the lightening of the dharma, showering the rain of the dharma, enacting the gift of the dharma, and by the constant sound of the dharma enlightening the many mundane realms.

The bodhisattva's radiant light universally illuminates immeasurable buddha lands, making the entirety of all the realms quake in six ways, encompassing even Māra's world to shake Māra's palace halls. The horde of demons are terrified and all surrender to conversion without exception. The net of obstructions are sundered, false views quenched, mental afflictions dispelled, the gutters of desire flushed, and the castle of the dharma safeguarded. The gate of the dharma is swung open and the impurities are cleansed revealing a lustrous purity. The bodhisattva's light illuminates the buddha-dharma, displaying the way to true transformation.

The bodhisattva enters various lands for alms, receiving all manner of food offerings that virtue may be accumulated, and revealing themselves as fields of merit. Wishing to proclaim the dharma, the bodhisattva manifests a joyous smile, and through the various medicines of the dharma, the bodhisattva cures the three sufferings. The bodhisattva reveals the immeasurable virtue of aspiring for enlightenment, and bestows on the other bodhisattvas the prediction of obtaining supreme perfect enlightenment. The bodhisattva manifests ultimate transcendence from this world, but the bodhisattva's salvation of others is without limit having extinguished the many contaminations and planted the various roots of virtue. Thus they are endowed with virtues of a sublimity and wonder difficult to measure.

The bodhisattvas traverse various buddha lands universally revealing the path of the doctrine. The religious practices they perform are pure without blemish. Like a conjurer, they manifest for the sentient beings various guises, becoming a man or a woman, there being no form they cannot take, and having mastered their studies, they can transform anything at will. Moreover, all these bodhisattvas are such as this.

They have studied the entirety of the dharma, mastered it thoroughly, and dwell in it securely, and there are none they do not edify. They all universally manifest themselves in innumerable buddha lands where, with neither arrogance nor self-indulgence, do they compassionately relieve the suffering of sentient beings. Such as this are they completely endowed with the entirety of the dharma.

The doctrine of the bodhisattva, they have penetrated thoroughly the essentials and subtleties, and their names spread universally to lead and edify sentient beings in the ten directions. Immeasurable buddhas, all of them together, safeguard the bodhisattvas, who have already attained the stage of dwelling in the abode of the buddha, and all stand in the position of great sages. The bodhisattvas use every means to broadly proclaim the dharma edified by the tathāgatas, and for the other bodhisattvas they become great teachers of the profound samādhi and wisdom by which to open the path for all sentient beings.

These bodhisattvas penetrate the essence of all phenomena, discern the nature of all sentient beings, and clearly perceive all the buddha lands, where they make offerings to all the buddhas manifesting themselves verily like a flash of lightening. The bodhisattvas are well learned in the net of fearlessness, and fully realize the illusory nature of all phenomena. They render asunder Māra's nets of the temptations and release the snares and fetters of the obstructions. They surpass the level of śrāvaka and pratyekabuddha, attaining the three samādhis of emptiness, non-form, and non-desire.

The bodhisattvas establish various expediencies, manifesting the three vehicles, and for the pratyekabuddhas and śrāvakas they manifest their ultimate transcendence of this world. However, for them there is nothing to accomplish and nothing to attain, no arising and no perishing, for they have attained the equanimity of the dharma. They are fully endowed with immeasurable powers of memory retention, hundreds of thousands of samādhis, and the faculties of wisdom. They enter the meditation of vast and universal tranquility, profoundly penetrating the bodhisattva storehouse of the dharma, attain the buddha flower garland samādhi, and elucidate and expound the entirety of the scriptural canon. The bodhisattvas dwell in the gate of profound samādhi, where they can presently see all the immeasurable buddhas, and in an instant of thought visit all without exception.

Moreover, the bodhisattvas rescue sentient beings in the tragic misery of the unfortunate realms, whether they are open to the path or not, and reveal true reality to them as appropriate. Having attained the wisdom of eloquence of the tathāgatas, they can penetrate the speech of all sentient beings and open the way to salvation for all. Having surpassed the mundane realm of phenomena, and their minds constantly dwelling in the path of transcendence, they have complete freedom in all things. For the sake of sentient beings they provide unsolicited friendship, shouldering these sentient beings and taking on their burdens.

The bodhisattvas, having received and maintaining the profound storehouse of the dharma from the tathāgatas, nurture the seed of buddha nature, ensuring its development without cessation. The bodhisattvas inspired with great compassion take mercy on sentient beings, expound the dharma with eloquent compassion, and bestow the dharma eye of insight. They close the paths to the three unfortunate destinies, and open the gates to the fortunate destinies. Without even needing to be asked, the bodhisattvas provide the dharma to the sentient beings, bestowing it with the love and respect a filial child feels for the father and mother, looking upon the sentient beings as their own selves.

Having accrued all these roots of good, all the bodhisattvas attain transcendence to the other shore. They have acquired the immeasurable virtues of all the buddhas, and their wisdom and brilliance is ineffable. Just such as this, these bodhisattvas, great sages, in incalculable numbers gathered at once at this assembly.

At that time, the World Honored One expressed extreme delight reflected in all of the Buddha's sense organs. The Buddha's form and hue were pure and immaculate, and the radiance of the Buddha's countenance was at an extraordinary peak. The Venerable Ānanda, perceiving the solemn import of the Buddha's expression, immediately rose from his seat, bared his right shoulder, knelt to the ground and joined his palms in reverence, addressing the Buddha, "Today the World Honored One emanates delight from all your sense organs, your form and hue are pure and immaculate and the radiance of the your countenance is at an extraordinary peak, verily as the reflection of a polished mirror penetrates surface and interior. Your majestic visage in its radiance is unsurpassed and immeasurable. I had yet to encounter such a wondrous marvel as just now.

"With respect, Great Sage, the thought occurs in my mind that, today the World Honored One dwells in the rare and exceptional dharma. Today the World Hero dwells in the abode of the buddhas. Today the Eye-of-the-World dwells in the conduct of a guiding master. Today the World Valiant One dwells in the most supreme path. Today the One-Honored-by-Celestials conducts the virtue of a Tathāgata. The buddhas of the past, present, and future, each contemplate all the other buddhas; is it not that now you, the Buddha, are also contemplating all the other buddhas? Is this why you radiate this extraordinary celestial light at this time?"

Thereupon, the World Honored One queried Ānanda, "I ask you, Ānanda, were you taught by the celestials to come ask this of the Buddha? Or was it your own wise insight that prompted you to ask about this extraordinary countenance?"

Ānanda replied to the Buddha, "There were no celestials who came to teach me this; I saw this myself, whereby I asked this question."

The Buddha said, "Well said, Ānanda. I am pleased with your question indeed. You have given rise to profound wisdom and true insightful speech that you have asked this sagacious question out of compassionate mindfulness of the sentient beings.

"The Tathāgata out of bottomless great mercy feels compassion for those in the three realms. For that reason, the Tathāgata has appeared in this world to illuminate the path of the teaching, wishing to rescue the sentient beings and endow them with the benefit of true reality. Even over immeasurable aeons, it is as difficult to directly encounter and see a buddha, as the udumbara flower that blossoms only on the rarest of occasion. Thus the question you now asked is of vast benefit for the edification of all the celestials and mortals.

"Ānanda, you must know, the wisdom of the Tathāgata, the Perfectly Awakened One, is difficult to measure, whereby guiding vast numbers of beings. The Tathāgata's wisdom and vision is without obstruction, nor can it be impeded. The buddha can preserve his life with a single meal for ten trillion aeons or even infinitely. Even so, the felicity of his senses will not deteriorate; the hue of his form will not change; and the radiance of his visage will not vary. This is because the Tathāgata's contemplation and wisdom is ultimate and eternal, enabling the free manifestation of the entirety of the dharma. Ānanda, listen well, and I will now explain in detail."

Ānanda responded, "I implore you to do so and will attend with joy."

The Buddha said to Ānanda, "Long ago in the far distant past of immeasurable, unfathomable, innumerable aeons ago, Dīpaṃkara Tathāgata appeared in this world and edified and delivered immeasurable sentient beings, who all attained the path, and then the Tathāgata transcended this world. Next there was a Tathāgata named Far-Reaching Light, then one named Moon Glow, then one named Sandalwood Fragrance, then one named Felicitous Mountain Sovereign, then one named Sumeru Heavenly Crown, then one named Sumeru Equal Brilliance, then one named Moon Hue, then one named Right Mindfulness, then one named Free-of-Defilements, then one named Non-Attachment, then one named Dragon Celestial, then one named Night Glow, then one named Peace Shining Peak, then one named Immovable Ground, then one named Lapis Lazuli Marvelous Blossom, then one named Lapis Lazuli Golden Hue, then one named Golden Treasury, then one named Flaming Light, then one named Flaming Root, then one named Earth-Shaking, then one named Moon Image, then one named Sun Voice, then one named Salvation Blossom, then one named Splendorous Glowing Radiance, then one named Ocean of Awakening Spiritual Powers, then one named Water Glow, then one named Grand Fragrance, then one named Free-of-Impurities, then one named Free-of-Distraught-Mind, then one named Treasure Flame, then one named Sublime Peak, then one named Intrepid Rising, then one named Virtue Maintaining Wisdom, then one named Obscuring Sun-and-Moon Light, then one named Sun-and-Moon Lapis Lazuli Light, then one named Unsurpassed Lapis Lazuli Light, then one named Supreme Chief, then one named Enlightenment Blossom, then one named Moon Radiance, then one named Sun Glow, then one named Blossom Hue Sovereign, then one named Water-Moon Light, then one named Free-of-Delusion, then one named Transcending Canopy of Conduct, then one named Pure Faith, then one named Felicitous Dwelling, then one named August Divinity, then one named Dharma Wisdom, then one named Phoenix Song, then one named Lion's Roar, then one named Dragon's Roar, and then one named World-Abiding. Just this way have all these buddhas now passed beyond."

"Then, there was a buddha named Lokeśvararāja, a thus-come one, worthy of offerings, perfectly awakened, accomplished in wisdom and conduct, well-gone, cognizant of the mundane world, supreme one, great subduer, master of celestials and mortals, the enlightened, world-honored one.

"At that time, there was a ruler of a land who heard this Buddha expound the dharma. His heart was filled with joy and he awakened to the aspiration for supreme perfect enlightenment. He renounced realm and abandoned throne to perform the ascetic practices of a śramaṇa, and was named Dharmākara. His intellectual brilliance and undaunted mettle surpassed all others in the world.

"Dharmākara proceeded to the place of Lokeśvararāja, bowed down in reverence at the Buddha's feet, circumambulated the Buddha three times on the right, knelt with palms together, and praised the Buddha in verse.

Glorious is the radiant visage,
Boundless in majestic power,

Like a blazing light
That has no equal.

The sun, the moon, and the maṇijewel
With marvelous light of flaming brilliance,
Are still all paled to obscurity
Akin to the darkness of black ink.

The comely visage of the Buddha
Supramundane and incomparable;
Your grand voice of perfect enlightenment
Reverberates throughout the ten directions.

Observance of the precepts, learning, devotional practices,
Samādhi, and wisdom
Peerless are these majestic virtues of the Buddha,
Outstanding and exceptional.

In profound clarity, does the Buddha contemplate
The ocean of the dharma of all the buddhas;
To the boundless depths, the farthest reaches,
The Buddha masters its deepest profundity.

Ignorance, desire, and wrath
Are forever absent from the World Honored One.
The valor of a lion among men,
Your divine virtue is immeasurable.
Far-reaching is your merit;
Your wisdom deep and sublime.
Your radiant light, awesome in form,
Shakes thousands of realms.

I vow to become a buddha
Like you, Sovereign of the Sacred Dharma,
To transcend over birth and death,
That none not attain emancipation.

My generosity, self-restraint,
Observance of the precepts, forbearance, and devotional practices,
Likewise samādhi and wisdom,

Will be supreme.

I vow to attain buddhahood,
Practicing constantly to fulfill this vow,
That all those in fear and anguish
May find great peace.

Should there be buddhas,
Of hundreds of thousands of millions of ten thousands,
Innumerable great sages
As many as the sands of the Ganges,

Offerings made to every one,
Of these many buddhas,
Still would be incomparable to seeking the way,
Resolutely without falter.

Though, like the sands of the Ganges,
All the buddha realms,
Are also incalculable,
Lands without number,

My light will illuminate them throughout,
Pervading all these various lands;
Such will be my devotional practices,
And my majestic power unfathomable.

When I have become a buddha,
First among all shall be my land;
The beings there of rare excellence,
And the seat of practice supreme.

My land will verily be a nirvana
Incomparable to any other.
I shall take compassion on them
And deliver all sentient beings.

Those from the ten directions,
Who come to be born in my land,
With hearts glad and pure,

Reach my land to find peace and serenity.

Buddha, I ask of you,
Accept my testimony and bear witness
As I pledge my vow before you
To dedicate my strength to this aspiration.

World Honored Ones of the ten directions,
Whose wisdom is without impediment,
May you Honored Ones forever
Know my sincere intent,

That though my body may remain
In the midst of suffering and hardship,
I will endeavor in this task,
Enduring to the end without regret."

The Buddha said to Ānanda, "Dharmākara, after having expounded this verse, addressed Lokeśvararāja Buddha, 'Thus, World Honored One, I have awakened to the aspiration for supreme perfect enlightenment, and I would ask the Buddha to give an expansive account of the scriptural dharma, then will I perform practices, select and adopt from the buddha lands the pure and pristine adornments of immeasurable wondrous lands. May that I, while in this world, quickly become perfectly enlightened and remove the many roots of the suffering of birth and death.'"

The Buddha said to Ānanda, "Then Lokeśvararāja Buddha said to Dharmākara, 'The performance of practices such as these to adorn a buddha land, you must already know yourself.'

"Dharmākara said to the Buddha, 'This is vast and profound, and not within my sphere of knowledge. Thus I would ask of you, World Honored One, to broadly expand on the practices by which the Tathāgata Buddhas purify their lands. Once I hear this, I will perform the practices as explained to fulfill my vow.'

"At that time, Lokeśvararāja Buddha knew the height of Dharmākara's wisdom and the vast profoundness of the intent of his vow, whereby the Buddha then expounded the doctrine for Dharmākara saying, 'If, for example, there was a great sea, a single person with a ladle would over a period of many aeons eventually empty it to the bottom and so obtain its wondrous treasures, just so would a person who endeavored in sincere intent, seeking the path without falter, obtain its realization. What vow could fail to be obtained?'

"At which, Lokeśvararāja Buddha then expansively explained twenty one billion buddha lands, the good and bad of the celestials and mortals, and the refinements and deficiencies of those lands, and in accord with Dharmākara's wish, manifested them all before him. Then Dharmākara, having heard the explanation of the Buddha of the adorned and purified lands and seen them all manifested before him, made an unsurpassed supreme vow. His mind tranquil and his intent without attachment, there were none equal to him in any world. For five full aeons, he considered and selected the pure practices for the adornment of a buddha land."

Ānanda asked the Buddha, "What was the lifespan of Lokeśvararāja and that land?"

The Buddha answered, "That Buddha's lifespan was forty-two aeons. During that time, Dharmākara selected pure practices from among twenty one billion wondrous buddha lands. After having finished this endeavor, Dharmākara proceeded to the place of Lokeśvararāja Buddha, bowed down in reverence at the Buddha's feet, circumambulated the Buddha three times, clasped palms together, stood before the Buddha and said, 'World-Honored One, I have selected the pure practices for the adornment of a buddha land.'

"Then Lokeśvararāja Buddha said to Dharmākara, 'Now you should expound them. It is time for them to be known. Proclaim them to the joy of the entire assembly. When the bodhisattvas have heard this, they will perform the practices of this dharma, and as a result fulfill immeasurable great vows.'

"Dharmākara said to the Buddha, 'Here then, lend me your ear as I expound my vows in detail.'

1. After I have attained buddhahood, should my land have hells, hungry ghosts, or beasts, then may I not attain perfect enlightenment.

2. After I have attained buddhahood, should any of the mortals or celestials in my land, who after their life has ended, again return to these three unfortunate paths, then may I not attain perfect enlightenment.

3. After I have attained buddhahood, should the mortals and celestials in my land all not have a true gold complexion, then may I not attain perfect enlightenment.

4. After I have attained buddhahood, should the mortals and celestials in

my land all not be of the same form and complexion, or should there be those more attractive or unsightly, then may I not attain perfect enlightenment.

5. After I have attained buddhahood, should the mortals and celestials in my land not be fully cognizant of their past lives, and not have knowledge of events extending back for hundreds of thousands of hundred millions of vast numbers of aeons, then may I not attain perfect enlightenment.

6. After I have attained buddhahood, should the mortals and celestials in my land not attain the divine eye, and not be able to see extending to hundreds of thousands of hundred millions of vast numbers of buddha lands, then may I not attain perfect enlightenment.

7. After I have attained buddhahood, should the mortals and celestials in my land not attain the divine ear, and not be able to hear the expounding of the dharma extending to hundreds of thousands of hundred millions of vast numbers of buddhas, and not be able to retain them all, then may I not attain perfect enlightenment.

8. After I have attained buddhahood, should the mortals and celestials in my land not attain the wisdom of seeing into the hearts of others, and not know the hearts and thoughts of sentient beings extending to hundreds of thousands of hundred millions of vast numbers of buddha lands, then may I not attain perfect enlightenment.

9. After I have attained buddhahood, should the mortals and celestials in my land not attain divine feet, and not be able in a single thought to traverse extending to over hundreds of thousands of hundred millions of vast numbers of buddha lands, then may I not attain perfect enlightenment.

10. After I have attained buddhahood, should the mortals and celestials in my land, if having given rise to deluded thoughts, have these become attached to their person, then may I not attain perfect enlightenment.

11. After I have attained buddhahood, should the mortals and celestials in my land not dwell in the assembly assured of enlightenment and not attain final transcendence without fail, then may I not attain perfect enlightenment.

12. After I have attained buddhahood, should my radiant light have a limit and not extend to illuminate hundreds of thousands of hundred millions of vast numbers of buddha lands, then may I not attain perfect enlightenment.

13. After I have attained buddhahood, should my lifespan have a limit and not extend to hundreds of thousands of hundred millions of vast numbers of aeons, then may I not attain perfect enlightenment.

14. After I have attained buddhahood, should the śrāvakas in my land be

of a calculable amount, even should the śrāvakas and pratyekabuddhas of three thousand, great thousand realms together calculate for hundreds of thousands of aeons and be able to know their numbers, then may I not attain perfect enlightenment.

15. After I have attained buddhahood, the mortals and celestials in my land shall have a lifespan of limitless amount, except for those who have limited their lifespans in accordance with their vows. Should this not be so, then may I not attain perfect enlightenment.

16. After I have attained buddhahood, should the mortals and celestials in my land even hear of anything "not virtuous," then may I not attain perfect enlightenment.

17. After I have attained buddhahood, should the immeasurable numbers of buddhas from the realms of the ten directions, each and every one of them, not praise and proclaim my name, then may I not attain perfect enlightenment.

18. After I have attained buddhahood, should any of the sentient beings in the ten directions, who aspire in all sincerity and faith wishing to be born in my land, recite the Buddha's name even ten times and not be born there, then may I not attain perfect enlightenment, with the exception of those who have committed the five grave offenses or maligned the true dharma.

19. After I have attained buddhahood, should any of the sentient beings in the ten directions awaken to the aspiration for enlightenment, practice meritorious virtue sincerely aspiring to be born in my land, and when their life comes to an end, should I surrounded by my entourage not appear before them, then may I not attain perfect enlightenment.

20. After I have attained buddhahood, should any of the sentient beings in the ten directions upon hearing my name, contemplate my land, plant the roots of virtue, and transfer their merit with a sincere mind wishing to be born in my land, and this not be realized, then may I not attain perfect enlightenment.

21. After I have attained buddhahood, should the mortals and celestials in my land, not each be fully endowed with the thirty-two major marks of a great personage, then may I not attain perfect enlightenment.

22. After I have attained buddhahood, should bodhisattvas from buddha lands in the other directions be born in my land, they shall unfailingly culminate in the stage of single rebirth—except for those who have made an original vow to transform freely, for the sake of sentient beings, to don their

vows like armor, accumulate the roots of virtue to liberate all beings, traverse the many buddha lands and practice the conduct of a bodhisattva, make offerings in homage to the buddhas and tathāgatas of the ten directions, edify immeasurable sentient beings as many as the sands of the Ganges, and establish them on the path to supreme perfect enlightenment. They shall transcend the ordinary bodhisattva stages of practice, and they shall practice the virtues of Samantabhadra manifested before them. Should this not be so, then may I not attain perfect enlightenment.

23. After I have attained buddhahood, should the bodhisattvas in my land, by the spiritual powers of the Buddha, make offerings to the many buddhas, and in the space of the first meal of the day, not extend even to innumerable immeasurable vast numbers of buddha lands, then may I not attain perfect enlightenment.

24. After I have attained buddhahood, should the bodhisattvas in my land, appear before the buddhas to manifest their roots of virtue, and wish for offerings to pay homage, and these not be as wished, then may I not attain perfect enlightenment.

25. After I have attained buddhahood, should the bodhisattvas in my land not be able to expound the dharma with complete wisdom, then may I not attain perfect enlightenment.

26. After I have attained buddhahood, should the bodhisattvas in my land not attain the adamantine body of the vajra Nārāyaṇa, then may I not attain perfect enlightenment.

27. After I have attained buddhahood, the mortals and celestials in my land, and all its myriad aspects, shall be ethereally pure and radiantly beautiful. Their forms and colors shall be highly distinguished, of utter subtlety and extreme refinement that cannot be enumerated. Should the sentient beings, even if having attained divine sight, be able to clearly discern all the details and enumerate their names, then may I not attain perfect enlightenment.

28. After I have attained buddhahood, should the bodhisattvas in my land, extending even to those yet of small merit, not be able to see the tree of enlightenment in all its immeasurable glowing colors with a height of four million leagues, then may I not attain perfect enlightenment.

29. After I have attained buddhahood, should the bodhisattvas in my land receive and read the scriptures of the dharma, and not attain eloquence and wisdom to repeat them verbatim, recite them from memory, and elucidate

them for others, then may I not attain perfect enlightenment.

30. After I have attained buddhahood, should the bodhisattvas in my land have any limit in wisdom and eloquence, then may I not attain perfect enlightenment.

31. After I have attained buddhahood, the pristine purity of my land, in every facet, shall reflect the sight of all the immeasurable innumerable unfathomable buddha worlds of the ten directions, just as the image of one's face appears in a clear mirror. Should this not be so, then may I not attain perfect enlightenment.

32. After I have attained buddhahood, all the palaces and pavilions, pools and streams, blossoms and trees in my land from earth to sky shall in all their myriad aspects have immeasurable varieties of jewels and one hundred thousand different fragrances. Their harmonious blend, decorative splendor, and rare magnificence shall surpass those of mortals and celestials. The fragrances shall universally waft throughout the worlds of the ten directions to inspire the bodhisattvas and śrāvakas in their practice of the buddha conduct. Should this not be so, then may I not attain perfect enlightenment.

33. After I have attained buddhahood, should any of the kinds of sentient beings in all the immeasurable unfathomable buddha worlds of the ten directions be embraced by my radiant light and their body touched by it, they shall become supple and genial in body and mind, surpassing that of mortals and celestials. Should this not be so, then may I not attain perfect enlightenment.

34. After I have attained buddhahood, should any kind of sentient being in all the immeasurable unfathomable buddha worlds of the ten directions hear my name, and not attain the bodhisattva insight of the non-arising of phenomena and the many profound dhāraṇīs, then may I not attain perfect enlightenment.

35. After I have attained buddhahood, should there be any woman in all the immeasurable unfathomable buddha worlds of the ten directions who hears my name, rejoices with ready faith, awakens to the aspiration for enlightenment, and deplores the afflictions of her female body, yet after her life has ended is again formed in the image of a woman, then may I not attain perfect enlightenment.

36. After I have attained buddhahood, should any of the host of bodhisattvas in all the immeasurable unfathomable buddha worlds of the ten

directions hear my name, after their life has ended, they shall constantly practice the celibate discipline of eliminating desire until they accomplish the path to become a buddha. Should this not be so, then may I not attain perfect enlightenment.

37. After I have attained buddhahood, should any of the celestials and mortals in all the immeasurable unfathomable buddha worlds of the ten directions hear my name, prostrate their entire body to the ground, bow their heads in respect, rejoice in ready faith, and practice the bodhisattva conduct, by all celestials and mortals shall they be revered. Should this not be so, then may I not attain perfect enlightenment.

38. After I have attained buddhahood, should the mortals and celestials in my land wish to attain clothing, they need only imagine it, and it shall be realized, and their bodies shall be naturally clothed in magnificent robes which accord with the dharma, such as would be applauded by the buddhas. Should these need sewing, dyeing, or cleaning, then may I not attain perfect enlightenment.

39. After I have attained buddhahood, should the state of beatitude obtained by the mortals and celestials in my land not be as that of monastics who have eliminated the defilements, then may I not attain perfect enlightenment.

40. After I have attained buddhahood, should the bodhisattvas in my land wish to see at will the immeasurable purely adorned buddha lands of the ten directions, when they make such a wish, then in every jewel tree shall the sight be reflected, just as the image of one's face appears in a clear mirror. Should this not be so, then may I not attain perfect enlightenment.

41. After I have attained buddhahood, should any of the host of bodhisattvas of buddha lands in the other directions hear my name and from thence to attaining buddhahood not be perfectly endowed with all the sense organs, then may I not attain perfect enlightenment.

42. After I have attained buddhahood, should any of the host of bodhisattvas of buddha lands in the other directions hear my name, they shall in all aspects attain the samādhi of pure emancipation, and while dwelling in that samādhi state, shall be able in an instant of thought to make offerings to immeasurable unfathomable numbers of buddhas and world honored ones without losing their concentration. Should this not be so, then may I not attain perfect enlightenment.

43. After I have attained buddhahood, should any of the host of

bodhisattvas of buddha lands in the other directions hear my name, after their life has ended, they shall be born in a venerable family. Should this not be so, then may I not attain perfect enlightenment.

44. After I have attained buddhahood, should any of the host of bodhisattvas of buddha lands in the other directions hear my name, they shall leap with joy, practice the bodhisattva conduct, and become endowed with the roots of virtue. Should this not be so, then may I not attain perfect enlightenment.

45. After I have attained buddhahood, should any of the host of bodhisattvas of buddha lands in the other directions hear my name, they shall in all aspects attain the samādhi of universal correspondence, and dwell in that samādhi state, from whence until becoming a buddha, shall be able to constantly see all the immeasurable unfathomable numbers of buddhas. Should this not be so, then may I not attain perfect enlightenment.

46. After I have attained buddhahood, should the bodhisattvas in my land wish to hear the dharma, exactly according to what they wish, they shall naturally attain the hearing of it. Should this not be so, then may I not attain perfect enlightenment.

47. After I have attained buddhahood, should any of the host of bodhisattvas of buddha lands in the other directions hear my name, and not immediately attain the stage of non-retrogression, then may I not attain perfect enlightenment.

48. After I have attained buddhahood, should any of the host of bodhisattvas of buddha lands in the other directions hear my name, and not immediately attain the first, second, and third insights of the dharma, and not attain a state of non-retrogression for the various dharmas of the buddhas, then may I not attain perfect enlightenment.

The Buddha said to Ānanda, "Once Dharmākara had expounded these vows, he then expounded in verse.

'I have established world-surpassing vows;
And will assuredly reach the unsurpassed path.
Should these vows not be fulfilled,
Then I pledge not to become perfectly awakened.

'Should I, for immeasurable aeons,
Not become a great benefactor,

Universally relieve the suffering of impoverishment,
Then I pledge not to become perfectly awakened.

'When I fulfill the path of the Buddha,
The sound of my name shall transcend the ten directions
Should it not be heard to the utmost limits,
Then I pledge not to become perfectly awakened.

Through the severing of desire, profound mindfulness,
Pure wisdom, and practicing the conduct of celibacy,
I will intently pursue the unsurpassed path,
And become a teacher of celestials and mortals.
'A buddha's divine power produces a great light,
Universally illuminating lands without end,
Dispelling the darkness of the three hindrances,
And providing deliverance from a host of perils and calamities.

'The eye of wisdom will be opened,
Eliminating the dark of blindness,
Cordoning shut the unfortunate paths,
And providing passage to the gate of fortunate destiny.

'Fully endowed with all the virtues and accomplishments,
The buddha's majestic radiance will extend to the ten directions,
Overwhelming the combined light of the sun and moon,
Eclipsing the celestial lights into invisibility.

'A buddha opens the treasury of the dharma for the many,
Widely distributes the buddha's wealth of merit,
And at a great assembly,
Always expounds the dharma with a lion's roar.

'By making offerings to all the buddhas,
Becoming endowed with the many roots of virtue,
Fulfilling each vow and perfecting wisdom,
A buddha becomes a valiant of the three mundane realms.

'Thus, the unimpeded wisdom of a buddha
Will be transmitted, leaving nowhere not illuminated.
I vow that the power of my virtue and wisdom

Be as that of the most superb Venerable One.

'If these vows are to be realized,
May the entire world quake in response,
And from the sky, may the various celestial beings,
Rain down marvelous flowers.'"

The Buddha said to Ānanda, "When Dharmākara finished expounding this verse, at that moment, the earth quaked universally in six ways. The celestials rained marvelous flowers, which fluttered down from above. Song appeared spontaneously out of nowhere to proclaim in verse, 'Your attainment of supreme perfect enlightenment is definitely assured.'

"At this, Dharmākara completed his endeavor in making these vows, which were true and unfailing, and aspired for the profound quiescence that transcends this world.

"Ānanda, at that time, before the Buddha and the great assembly of celestials including Māra and Brahma and the Dragon King with the rest of the Eight Protective Deities, did Dharmākara pronounce these grand vows. Having established these vows, Dharmākara dedicated himself with single intent to the ethereal adornment of a land of marvel. Through his practices, Dharmākara would form this buddha land to be infinitely vast, supreme in its special marvels. He would establish it to be everlasting, without deterioration or change.

"For an unfathomable nearly infinite number of aeons, did Dharmākara accumulate and cultivate immeasurable virtuous practices of the bodhisattva. The consciousness of desire, the consciousness of hatred, and the consciousness of malevolence did not arise. Nor did thoughts of desire, hatred, or malevolence occur. Nor did he become attached to the concepts of form, sound, smell, taste, or touch. He achieved the power of forbearance, did not reckon any suffering, was satisfied with few needs, and was without desire, enmity, or delusion. His samādhi was of constant serenity and his wisdom unobstructed. He harbored no falsehood or flattery in his heart, his visage was serene and his words kind, and he intuited the thoughts of others and responded accordingly.

"Dharmākara endeavored with fearless valor and unwavering intent, devoting himself to the pursuit of the pure dharma, whereby to benefit the multitude of living beings. He revered the three treasures and paid obeisance to his masters and superiors. Thus, did he greatly adorn his virtue, accomplish the bodhisattva practices, and enable living beings to acquire virtue and merit. Dwelling in the dharma of emptiness, non-form, and non-desire, with no formation and no arising, he perceived all phenomena to be like a mirage. He refrained from grievous words and what would be injurious to himself, or injurious to others, or mutually injurious; and practiced only good words and what would be of benefit for himself, or of benefit for others, or of mutual benefit for both.

"Dharmākara renounced kingdom and discarded throne, removed himself from wealth and pleasure, practiced the six pāramitās himself, and taught others so that they could practice. He accumulated merit and amassed virtue for an immeasurable number of aeons. Wherever he was born, in accord with what was desired, an immeasurable storehouse of treasures naturally appeared in response. He converted and securely established immeasurable living beings so that they would dwell on the path of supreme perfect enlightenment.

"At times, he became an elder, a lay-devotee of the merchant caste, a Brahmana, or a chancellor. At other times, he became a king of the warrior caste or a Cakravartin king, or yet a king of the six realms of desire, or even a king of the Brahman heaven. Always did he make the four kinds of offerings and pay homage to all the buddhas.

"His virtues, such as these, cannot be sufficiently praised. The breath from his mouth was as fragrant as a blue water lily and the pores of his body emitted the scent of sandalwood. This fragrance universally perfumed immeasurable worlds. His visage and hue were perfect and he was endowed with all the major and minor buddha marks, which were particularly refined. From his hands there was a constant flow of endless treasures, robes and garments, food and drink, marvelous flowers and fragrances, canopies and banners, and objects of adornment. The many objects such as these surpassed that of celestials, and moreover he could attain any object at will."

Ānanda said to the Buddha, "Has Dharmākara already become a buddha and transcended to nirvana? Or has he not yet become a buddha? Or is he even now present?"

The Buddha replied to Ānanda, "Dharmākara has now already become the Buddha of Infinite Life and is present in the west, ten trillion buddha realms away. That buddha realm is called Serenity and Beatitude."

Ānanda then asked, "How much time has passed since this buddha fulfilled the path?"

The Buddha said, "About ten aeons have passed since becoming a buddha.

"This buddha's land is naturally of seven jewels: gold, silver, aquamarine beryl, coral, amber, white-shell, and cornelian. Together they form the ground, boundless in width and breadth, immeasurable in limit and scope. The jewels reflect each other in a kaleidoscope of refraction, in radiant brilliance of exquisite beauty. Their pure adornment surpasses that of all the worlds in the ten directions. The specter of these jewels is just as that of the sixth heaven.

"Moreover, this land has no Mount Sumeru, no ring of adamantine iron-mountains, nor any mountain whatsoever. Furthermore, there are no seas large or small, nor gorges or valleys. But by the spiritual powers of the Buddha, if it is wished that they be seen, then they can be seen. In addition, there are no hells, hungry ghosts, or beasts, nor any of the unfortunate destinies. Also, the four seasons of spring, fall, winter, and summer do not exist. It is neither cold nor hot, but rather always temperate and mild."

Then Ānanda said to the Buddha, "World Honored One, if in that land there is no Mount Sumeru, then where do the Four Deva Kings and those of Heaven of the Thirty-three Devas reside?"

The Buddha said to Ānanda, "Those of Yama's Heaven, extending to include even those of the Heaven of the Most Rarefied Form, where do they all reside?"

Ānanda submitted to the Buddha, "The karmic effect of actions and conduct is ineffable."

The Buddha said to Ānanda, "The karmic effect of actions and conduct is indeed ineffable, and moreover are the realms of the buddhas ineffable. Thus, all these sentient beings reside on the ground of their actions and conduct through the power of their virtue and good acts."

Ānanda said to the Buddha, "I did not doubt this dharma, but only to remove such doubts for the sake of future sentient beings, have I asked this question."

The Buddha said to Ānanda, "The majestic and divine radiant light of the Buddha of Infinite Life is foremost and most supreme; the radiant lights of all the other buddhas cannot even approach it. There are buddha lights which illuminate a hundred buddha realms, or others a thousand buddha realms. Furthermore, others yet illuminate buddha lands in the eastern direction as many as the sands of the Ganges, and to the directions of the south, west, and north, the four points between, and the directions above and below, all likewise so. Also there are buddha lights which illuminate for seven feet, or for one yojana, or two, or three, or four, or five yojanas, in this way, increasing in degrees until illuminating an entire buddha land.

"For this reason, this Buddha of Infinite Life is also known as the Buddha of Immeasurable Light, Buddha of Boundless Light, Buddha of Unobstructed Light, Buddha of Unopposed Light, Buddha of Flaming Sovereign Light, Buddha of Pristine Pure Light, Buddha of Joyous Light, Buddha of the Light of Wisdom, Buddha of Unceasing Light, Buddha of Inconceivable Light, Buddha of Ineffable Light, and Buddha of Light Surpassing Sun and Moon.

"Those sentient beings who encounter this light will have the three hindrances eliminated, become amenable in body and mind, leap with joy, and their hearts will give rise to good. Should they suffer hardship in the three realms of defilement, when they see this radiant light, they will all attain relief and not again suffer this pain. After their life has ended, they will all obtain release.

"The radiant light of the Buddha of Infinite Life is dazzling brilliant, illuminating all the buddha lands of the ten directions, and there is nowhere it is not heard of. It is not just I who now praises this radiant light, all the myriad buddhas, śrāvakas, pratyekabuddhas, the entire assembly of bodhisattvas, all of them likewise praise and glorify it in the same way.

"Should there be sentient beings who hear of this radiant light, its majestic and divine virtue, and declare it day and night from the bottom of their hearts without cease, in accordance with their aspiration will they attain birth in this land, where their virtue will then be praised and glorified in union by all of the bodhisattvas and śrāvakas of the great assembly. Then afterwards when they have achieved the Buddhist path, all the buddhas and bodhisattvas of the ten directions will universally extol their radiant light in the same manner as just now."

The Buddha said, "Were I to expound the radiant light of the Buddha of Infinite Life, the subtleties of its majestic power and glorious splendor, day and night for an entire aeon, I still could not fully accomplish it."

The Buddha said to Ānanda, "The Buddha of Infinite Life has a lifespan so long lasting that it cannot be calculated. You should rather know this. If, for instance, immeasurable sentient beings from the worlds in the ten directions, all attained a mortal body and were able to become a śrāvaka or a pratyekabuddha, and they all gathered together and meditated whole heartedly with their combined mental powers for hundreds of thousands of ten thousands of aeons, calculating in union the immense vast numbers of lifespan, still they could not reach the end and know its limits. The length of the lifespan of the assembly of śrāvakas, bodhisattvas, celestials, and mortals is again such as this; neither by calculation nor by analogy is it knowable.

"Moreover in regard to the śrāvakas and bodhisattvas, their numbers are hardly measurable and cannot be expressed. They are vested with supramundane wisdom and powers. They have complete freedom over their majestic powers and can hold the entire universe in the palm of their hand."

The Buddha said to Ānanda, "The number of śrāvakas gathered at that Buddha's first assembly is incalculable, and likewise for the bodhisattvas. Now even if those like the great Maudgalyāyana in immeasurable numbers of hundreds of thousands of ten thousands of hundred millions should count together for incalculable vast numbers of aeons, even onto transcending into extinction, still they would be unable to reach the end of these many numbers. Should there, for instance, be a great sea immeasurably deep and wide, and should there be a person with one strand of hair reduced to a hundredth of its size, and that fraction of a hair used to scoop a drop from that sea, what do you think? How much greater would that great sea be than that single drop?"

Ānanda said to the Buddha, "A great sea compared to that single drop of water would be of an amount that neither by the calculations of astronomers nor by the metaphors of rhetoricians could be knowable."

The Buddha said to Ānanda, "Even if those like Maud-galyāyana were for hundreds of thousands of ten thousands of hundred millions of vast numbers of aeons to count the śrāvakas and bodhisattvas of that first assembly, the numbers they would know would merely be a single drop out of the unknowable drops of water in a great sea."

"Moreover, in that land there are trees of seven jewels, which fill the entire surroundings of that realm. There are trees of gold, and of silver, lapis lazuli, crystal, coral, cornelian, and mother-of-pearl. There are also trees composed in a combination of two or three jewels, extending up to seven jewels. There are trees of gold with leaves, flowers, and fruits of silver and trees of silver with leaves, flowers, and fruits of gold. There are trees of lapis lazuli with leaves, flowers, and fruits of crystal and trees of quartz with the leaves, flowers, and fruits all likewise of lapis lazuli. There are trees of coral with leaves, flowers, and fruits of cornelian and trees of cornelian with the leaves, flowers, and fruits all likewise of lapis lazuli. There are trees of mother-of-pearl with the leaves, flowers, and fruits all likewise of a multitude of jewels.

"There are also jewel trees with purple-gold forming the roots, white-silver forming the trunks, lapis lazuli forming the limbs, quartz forming the branches, coral forming the leaves, cornelian forming the flowers, and mother-of-pearl forming the fruits. There are jewel trees with white-silver forming the roots, lapis lazuli forming the trunks, quartz forming the limbs, coral forming the branches, cornelian forming the leaves, mother-of-pearl forming the flowers, and purple-gold forming the fruits. There are jewel trees with lapis lazuli forming the roots, quartz forming the trunks, coral forming the limbs, cornelian forming the branches, mother-of-pearl forming the leaves, purple-gold forming the flowers, and white-silver forming the fruits. There are jewel trees with quartz forming the roots, coral forming the trunks, cornelian forming the limbs, mother-of-pearl forming the branches, purple-gold forming the leaves, white-silver forming the flowers, and lapis lazuli forming the fruits. There are jewel trees with coral forming the roots, cornelian forming the trunks, mother-of-pearl forming the limbs, purple-gold forming the branches, white-silver forming leaves, lapis lazuli forming the flowers, and quartz forming the fruits. There are jewel trees with cornelian forming the roots, mother-of-pearl forming the trunks, purple-gold forming the limbs, white-silver forming the branches, lapis lazuli forming the leaves, quartz forming the flowers, and coral forming the fruits. There are jewel trees with mother-of-pearl forming the roots, purple-gold forming the trunks, white-silver forming the limbs, lapis lazuli forming the branches, quartz forming the leaves, coral forming the flowers, and cornelian forming the fruits.

"These jewel trees are planted in even rows, the trunks stretch up evenly, the limbs are arranged in even order, the leaves face out evenly, the flowers are distributed evenly, and the fruits are evenly dispersed. The splendorous colors, the glittering brilliance cannot be viewed in whole. When pure breezes arise, they give forth the five notes in a subtle pentatonic scale, which harmonize naturally.

"Moreover, the tree of enlightenment of the Buddha of Infinite Life's land is four million leagues in height, the roots fifty yojanas in circumference, and the branches and leaves extend two hundred thousand leagues in the four directions. All of its many jewels are naturally in harmony and it is adorned in splendor with the moon-glow maṇi jewel, the ocean-bearing-cakra jewel, the king of jewels. Hanging from between the branches are suspended jewel garlands of a billion various different colors and of immeasurable flaming light and limitless glowing brilliance, and hung above are rare and marvelous jewel nets. All of these adornments are manifested as desired.

"A delicate wind stirs to rustle the branches and leaves to produce immeasurable sounds and voices of the marvelous dharma. These voices flow throughout all the buddha lands universally. Those who hear these sounds attain the insight into the profound dharma and dwell in the stage of non-retrogression. Until they fulfill the Buddhist path, their sense organs such as the ear will perceive clearly without suffering impairment. Their eyes will see the hues, their eyes hear the sounds, their noses know the fragrance, their tongues taste the flavor, their bodies feel the light, and their minds grasp the substance of the dharmas. They will all attain the insight into the profound dharma and dwell in the stage of non-retrogression. Until they fulfill the Buddhist path, their six organs will perceive clearly without any malady or impairment.

"Ānanda, when the mortals and celestials of that land see that tree, they will attain the three insights into the dharma. The first of these is the insight of reality through hearing; the second is the insight of acceptance of reality; and the third is the insight of the non-arising of phenomenon. These are all made possible by the supernormal power of the Buddha of Infinite Life, through the power of the original vow, the power of the fulfillment of the vow, the power of the perspicuity of the vow, the power of the immutability of the vow, and the power of the perfection of the vow."

The Buddha said to Ānanda, "A sovereign of the mundane world has a hundred thousand forms of music. From a Cakravartin King proceeding up to the sixth heaven, the melodies of the musical arts of each world are progressively ten hundred thousand billion times superior to the former. Although the sixth heaven has myriad forms of melodies, it still is incomparable to the land of the Buddha of Infinite Life, in which even one of the melodies from the trees of seven jewels is still yet a hundred billion times superior. Furthermore, the myriad forms of musical arts occur naturally and moreover none of them fail to produce the sounds of the dharma. The music is clear and resonant, subtle and refined, the most superior of all the worlds in the ten directions.

"Moreover, the lecture halls, monk cells, palaces, and pavilions are all of seven jewels in ethereal adornment, and naturally formed by transformation. Furthermore, a host of pearls and radiant-moon maṇi jewels form a canopy that glistens like dewdrops and hangs as a covering above.

"Inside and outside, to the left and right are many bathing pools. Some are ten yojanas in size, some are twenty or thirty, extending even to a hundred thousand yojanas. For each, the length, width, and depth are all equal in dimension. They brim full with waters of the eight virtues, which are pure, fragrant, and have the flavor of nectar. The yellow-gold pools have bottoms of white-silver sand and the pools of white silver have bottoms of yellow-gold sand. The crystal pools have bottoms of lapis lazuli sand and the lapis lazuli pools have bottoms of crystal sand. The coral pools have bottoms of amber sand and the pools of amber have bottoms of coral sand. The mother-of-pearl pools have bottoms of cornelian sand and the cornelian pools have bottoms of mother-of-pearl sand. The white-jade pools have bottoms of purple-gold sand and the pools of purple-gold have bottoms of white-jade sand. There are also those composed in a combination of two or three jewels, extending up to seven jewels.

"On the banks of these pools are sandalwood trees, the blossoms and leaves of which drape down releasing a pleasant fragrance universally. Celestial blue water lilies, crimson lotuses, yellow water lilies, and white lotuses, glowing lush with various colors, spread out across the water.

"Should the bodhisattvas and śrāvakas enter these jewel pools and wish the water to soak their feet, then the water soaks their feet. Should they wish it to rise to their knees, then it rises to their knees. Should they wish it to rise to their waist, then it raises to their waist. Should they wish it to rise to their neck, then it rises to their neck. Should they wish it to shower their whole body, then naturally it showers their whole body. Should they wish the water to recede back as before, then it recedes back as before.

"The water is a perfect balance of hot and cold naturally adjusting as wished. It opens the spirit and soothes the body, washing away the impurities of the heart. The water is pure and lucid, sparkling and luminous, so pristine as to be almost immaterial. The jewel sands reflect from the bottom and there is no depth at which they are not illuminated. Subtle ripples flow out in rings across the surface, overlapping where the rings of ripples cross. Gently and quietly do they flow, neither too brisk nor too weak.

"The waves burble with immeasurable subtle voices, by which there are none who do not hear what they wish. At times the sound of the Buddha is heard, or the sound of the dharma is heard, or the sound of the saṃgha is heard. At times the sound of quiescence, or the sound of emptiness and non-self, or the sound of great mercy and compassion, or the sound of the pāramitās, or the sound of the ten powers, fearlessness, and the peerless characteristics of the Buddha, or the sound of supernormal powers, or the sound of non-effort, or the sound of non-arising and non-ceasing, or the sound of the insight of non-arising of phenomena, even extending to the sound of ordination by nectar anointment, and many more sounds such as these of the subtle dharma can be heard.

"They whose wishes are fulfilled by hearing these answering voices are immeasurably overjoyed. At which, then follows the substance of pristine purity in the severing of desires and the quiescence of true reality; then follows the dharma of the three treasures, ten powers, fearlessness, and the peerless characteristics of the Buddha; then follows spiritual powers and the path of the bodhisattva and śrāvaka. There is no word for the three realms of defilement and suffering; there are only the naturally arising sounds of euphoria. This is why that land is called Serenity and Beatitude.

"Ānanda, all those who achieve birth in that Buddha's land are fully endowed with such as pure complexions and bodies, sublime voices, spiritual powers, and virtue. Their palaces, garments, food and drink, many subtle blossoms and fragrances, and personal adornments are just as those that naturally occur in the sixth heaven. If they wish to eat, then seven-jewel dishes naturally appear before them, such as of gold and silver, lapis lazuli, mother-of-pearl, cornelian, coral, amber, and the radiant-moon maṇi jewel. In accordance with their thoughts, the plates are naturally laden with a hundred flavors of food and drink. However, though there is this food, it is not actually eaten. Rather, just by seeing the colors and smelling the aroma, they are naturally fully satiated with the sense of having eaten. They become relaxed and genial in body and mind with no attachment to the flavor. When finished, the dishes disappear, to then reappear at the next time.

"That buddha land is pristinely pure, peacefully tranquil, and of subtle pleasures, following on the unconditioned path of nirvana. All the śrāvakas, bodhisattvas, celestials, and mortals are of lofty brilliance in their wisdom, and fully accomplished in their spiritual powers. All are of the same kind, with no difference in form. Only as a remnant of their past are they called celestial or mortal. Their visage is perfected, surpassing this world in its marvel. Their complexion and hue are sublime; neither celestial nor mortal, all are naturally bestowed with a body empty of form, a body without limitation."

The Buddha said to Ānanda, "Should, for instance, there be in this world a person of beggarly circumstances set beside an emperor, how would they compare in appearance and demeanor?"

Ānanda said to the Buddha, "Such a person set beside an emperor, would be emaciated, unsightly, repugnant, and foul in comparison. A hundred thousand, ten thousand hundred million times, incalculably so, in no way would the person be comparable. This is because of the impoverishment and low caste of a person of beggarly circumstances, who has clothes that hardly cover the body and food only enough to keep alive. Suffering from cold and hunger, such a person is of just barely human circumstances.

"All such in their previous lives did not plant the roots of virtue, and were not charitable with their accumulated wealth. The more wealth they had, the more parsimonious they became, insatiably longing for more with a greed that was relentless. They performed no good deeds whatsoever, but rather piled up a mountain of evil actions. In this manner their life came to an end and their wealth and treasures were dispersed. What they had accumulated through great hardship only caused them further anguish, that in the end they had no gain, it all fruitlessly becoming the possessions of others. They had no good to rely on, no virtue to depend on. For this reason, when they died they fell into the unfortunate destinies, where they suffer at length. Once they have finished serving for their offenses and are released, they are born in the lowest circumstances, one of ignorance and inferiority, barely appearing to be of the same human species.

"The reason emperors in the mundane realm are especially exalted among mortals is because they all accumulated virtue in their previous lives. Wise and merciful, they dedicated themselves to charity; benevolent and kind, they saved others from suffering. Treading with sincerity, they practiced good and never contended with others. Thus when their life ended, their merit allowed them to attain the good path, and they ascended to birth in the heavens above, where they enjoyed felicity and bliss. Their accumulated good has a surplus of felicity that they are now able to become a mortal fortuitously born in a ruler's family, naturally respected and honored. Such are comely and upright and revered by the masses. They enjoy marvelous robes and rare delicacies as they wish. This is the result of the merit accrued in past lives."

The Buddha said to Ānanda, "It is as you say. An emperor, for instance, is revered among mortals and is upright in form and complexion, but when compared to a Cakravartin King is just as coarse and inferior as a person of beggarly circumstances beside an emperor. A Cakravartin King is dignified in appearance and especially refined, the foremost under heaven, but when compared to Indra, the celestial king of the Trāyastriṃśa heaven, is again unsightly, incomparably so by ten thousand, hundred million times. If then Indra is compared to the king of the sixth heaven, the difference would be incomparable by a hundred thousand, hundred million times. Then if the king of the sixth heaven was compared to the bodhisattvas and śrāvakas in the land of the Buddha of Infinite Life, in their radiant visage and comely hue, they would be incomparable by a hundred thousand, ten thousand hundred million times, incalculably so."

The Buddha said to Ānanda, "In accordance with the shape and hue of all the celestials and mortals in the land of the Buddha of Infinite Life, their garments, food and drink, flowers and fragrances, ornaments, parasols, banners, sublime melodies, the residences, palaces, and pavilions where they dwell are perfectly suited high and low, and large and small. Moreover, one jewel or two jewels, even extending up to an immeasurable host of jewels, are as they wish in accordance with their thoughts. Furthermore, marvelous cloths of many jewels are spread throughout on the ground for all the celestials and mortals to tread upon as they go forth. Nets of immeasurable jewels are hung throughout the buddha land, which have gold threads with pearls and a hundred thousand varieties of jewels of rare marvel intermingling in ethereal adornment. They cover the four quarters, hung with jewel bells, and their radiant colors and glowing brilliance are of an overwhelmingly ethereal beauty.

"Naturally, a wind of virtue quietly arises with subtle movement. This wind is temperate, neither hot nor cold, amenable in warmth and coolness, and neither too brisk or weak. It stirs the gauze nets and jewel trees giving rise to a melody of immeasurable subtle sounds of the dharma, and with it flows myriad genial and refined fragrances of virtue. For those who hear and smell this, naturally the hindrances do not arise, and they whose bodies are touched by the wind attain a state of beatitude such as the samādhi of cessation attained by monastics.

"Moreover, the breeze blows scattering the blossoms, spreading them out throughout the buddha land. Their colors are graduated in degrees so that they do not clash. They are soft, of lustrous light, and of fragrance that wafts long and pleasant. When stepped upon, they sink down four inches, but when the foot is raised, they recover just as before. When the blossoms are spent, the ground opens up and the blossoms disappear, for a pristine purity with no speck remaining. When the time comes, again the winds blow to scatter the blossoms, in this way repeated six times a day.

"Furthermore, a host of jewel lotus blossoms envelope and fill the land. Each individual jewel blossom has a hundred thousand hundred-million petals. The radiant light of these blossoms has immeasurable different colors. The blue colors have blue light; the white colors have white light; the ebony, yellow, vermillion, and purple colors also have lights of their colors. They are intensely bright and resplendently vivid, as radiantly brilliant as the sun and moon. Each individual blossom emits thirty-six hundred thousand hundred-million lights, and each individual light emits thirty-six hundred thousand hundred-million buddhas, whose bodies are of purple-gold hue, with buddha marks that are especially extraordinary. Each of these buddhas again emits a hundred thousand radiant lights universally to the ten directions, which expound the sublime and marvelous dharma. In this way, each of these buddhas sets immeasurable sentient beings securely on the true path of the buddha."

Part Two

The Buddha said to Ānanda, "Those sentient beings born in this land will all without exception dwell among those assured of enlightenment. Why is this? In this Buddha's Land, there are none who are destined to the unfortunate fates, and there are none of indeterminate destiny.

"All the buddhas, tathāgatas, in the ten directions, as numerous as the sands of the Ganges, together sing the praise of the majestic and divine virtue of the Buddha of Infinite Life, which is unfathomable. All those sentient beings who hear this Buddha's name, rejoice in faith, and recite this Buddha's name even once, dedicating their minds to transferring merit and aspiring to birth in that land, they will then achieve birth there and dwell in the stage of non-retrogression—except for those who commit the five grave offenses or malign the true dharma."

The Buddha said to Ānanda, "The celestials and mortals of the worlds in the ten directions who dedicate their minds aspiring to be born in that land are of three types of aspirants."

"The superior aspirants are those who forsake their homes, discard worldly desires, and become a śramaṇa renunciant. They awaken to the aspiration for enlightenment, dedicate themselves to reciting the name of the Buddha of Infinite Life, practice meritorious virtue, and aspire to be born in that land. For these sentient beings, when their life comes to an end, the Buddha of Infinite Life, accompanied by a great assembly, will appear right before them. Then they will follow this Buddha to achieve birth in that land, where they will be spontaneously born by transformation within a seven-jewel blossom. They will dwell in the stage of non-retrogression, with overwhelming wisdom, and free command of spiritual powers. For that reason Ānanda, if sentient beings wish to see the Buddha of Infinite Life in this world, they should awaken to the aspiration for supreme enlightenment, practice meritorious virtue, and aspire to be born in that land."

The Buddha said to Ānanda, "The intermediate aspirants are those among the humans and celestial deities of the worlds of the ten directions who dedicate their minds in aspiration to be born in that land, and though unable to practice as a śramaṇa renunciant and so cultivate great merit, should awaken to the aspiration for supreme enlightenment and single-mindedly recite the name of the Buddha of Infinite Life. They perform good, great and small, by upholding the precepts of abstinence, building Buddhist sculptures and pagodas, offering food to the śramaṇas, hanging banners, lighting torches, spreading flowers, and lighting incense. They aspire to be born in that land through the transference of this merit. At the end of their life, the Buddha of Infinite Life, as a transformed manifestation with the radiance and bodily marks of the Buddha's true form, attended by a great assembly, will appear before them. Then they will follow this transformed Buddha to achieve birth in that land and dwell in the stage of non-retrogression, with the merit and wisdom second to the superior aspirant."

The Buddha said to Ānanda, "The inferior aspirants are those among the humans and celestial deities of the worlds of the ten directions who dedicate their minds in aspiration to be born in that land, and though unable to form much merit, should awaken to the aspiration for supreme enlightenment and single-mindedly, even ten times, recite the name of the Buddha of Infinite Life, aspiring for birth in that land. When they hear this profound dharma, are overjoyed and readily have faith without doubts arising, and recite the name of this Buddha even once with a sincere mind, aspiring to be born in that land, then at the time of their death they will see this Buddha as in a dream and achieve birth. Their merit and wisdom will be second to the intermediate aspirant."

The Buddha said to Ānanda, "The majestic power of the Buddha of Infinite Life is unsurpassable. All the immeasurable, limitless, inconceivable buddhas, tathāgatas from the worlds of the ten directions praise the Buddha of Infinite Life without fail. Immeasurable, innumerable assemblies of bodhisattvas from the buddha lands in the eastern direction, as numerous as the sands of the Ganges, all come to visit the place of the Buddha of Infinite Life and pay reverence and make offerings, extending even to all of the bodhisattvas and śrāvakas in the great assembly. Having heard and received this teaching of the dharma, they then lead others to the Buddhist path. Likewise so it is in the south, west, north directions, as well as the intermediate directions, and the directions above and below."

Then the World Honored One expounded this in verse.

"From buddha lands of the east as
Numerous as the sands of the Ganges
Come bodhisattvas of those lands
To see this buddha of immeasurable enlightenment.

"Likewise for the south, west, and north, the points in between,
And those above and below,

Come the bodhisattvas of those lands
To see this buddha of immeasurable enlightenment.

"Everyone of these bodhisattvas
Each brings exquisite heavenly flowers,
Precious incense, and priceless garments
As offerings to this buddha of immeasurable enlightenment.
"They perform heavenly music in concert
Producing harmonious melody
To sing the praises of the Most Honored One
In offering to this buddha of immeasurable enlightenment:

"'You have fully attained spiritual powers and wisdom;
You have traversed through the gate of the profound dharma;
You possess a treasury of merit;
Your marvelous intelligence is incomparable.

"'Your wisdom like the sun illuminates the world,
Dispelling the clouds of birth and death.'
In reverence, the bodhisattvas circumambulate three times
And bow their heads to the ground before the Unsurpassed One.

"When they saw the adornment of the Pure Land,
It was unimaginably refined.
Wherefore they were profoundly inspired
And vowed to establish their own lands in this way.

"At which time, the Immeasurable One's
Countenance changed breaking into a smile.
Infinite light emitted from his mouth,
Illuminating all the lands in the ten directions.

"That light circumambulated the Buddha three times,
And then entered the crown of the Buddha's head.
The entire assembly of celestials and mortals,
All danced with joy.

"Then, the bodhisattva Avalokiteśvara,
Robes respectfully arranged and head bowed to the ground, inquired:
'Dear Buddha, why do you smile?

I implore you to explain its meaning.'

"The Buddha's voice, with the thunder and rumble of Brahma,
Resounded magnificently with the eight qualities:
'The prediction of future buddhahood for the bodhisattvas,
I will now explain. Listen with care.

"'All of the Bodhisattvas who have come from the ten directions,
I know of each of their vows,
That they have resolved to establish pure lands.
For them it is predicted that they will become buddhas.

"'Fully understanding all phenomena,
That are yet like a dream, illusion, or echo,
And fulfilling their marvelous vows,
They will assuredly establish a land like this one.

"'Knowing all phenomena instantly like a flash of lightening,
And endeavoring on the path of the bodhisattva,
They acquire the roots of merit.
For them it is predicted that they will become buddhas.

"'Thoroughly mastering the nature of all phenomena,
That all is empty and without substance,
They single-mindedly strive to establish a pure buddha land.
They will assuredly establish a land like this one.'

"All the buddhas exhort the bodhisattvas
To go and pay homage to the Buddha of the Land of Peace and
Provision:
'Listen to the dharma, joyously receiving and practicing it,
And quickly realize your own site of purity.'

"Once they have reached that adorned Pure Land,
They will soon acquire spiritual powers,
And from the Immeasurable One assuredly
Receive the prediction of future buddhahood and attain enlightenment.

"Through the power of the Buddha's original vow,
They who hear the name of the Buddha and aspire to achieve birth,

Will, each and every one, reach this Buddha's land
And spontaneously attain the stage of non-retrogression.

"The bodhisattvas make a sincere vow,
'I vow my land be no different,'
Constantly being mindful that 'I will deliver all sentient beings,
By revealing my name throughout the ten directions.'

"In order to present offerings to hundreds of millions of tathāgatas,
They will fly by transformation to various lands,
Pay homage, rejoice, and depart,
To return to the Land of Peace and Provision.

"Those without the roots of good,
Will fail to hear this sutra,
But those who are pure and maintain the precepts,
Can surely hear the true dharma.

"Those who have already encountered a World Honored One
Can now surely believe in this.
Hearing and receiving this practice in reverence,
They rejoice as though to leap with joy.

"Those who are arrogant, indolent, or lacking in devotion,
Find it difficult to believe in this dharma,
But those who encountered buddhas in past lives,
Joyfully listen to teachings such as this.

"Neither śrāvaka nor bodhisattva,
Can fathom the Sage's mind.
They are like those born blind,
Yet wishing to open the way for others.

"The wisdom of the Tathāgata is like the ocean,
Infinitely broad and deep.
Those of the two vehicles cannot fathom it;
Only the buddhas can clearly understand it.

"Even if all the people of the world,
With all the attainments to achieve the Buddhist path,

Acquired pure wisdom knowing the basis of emptiness,
And for a hundred million aeons tried to imagine the Buddha's wisdom,

"And even holding discursive meetings with all their might,
Until the end of their lives, they still would not understand
The Buddha's wisdom which is without limitation,
Such is its purity.
"It is difficult to obtain life,
And even more difficult to be born when a buddha is present.
It is difficult for people to have faith and wisdom.
If you hear this, endeavor to pursue it.

"If you hear the dharma and do not forget it,
Regard it with respect and reverence,
Then you will be my 'good friend.'
Therefore, you should awaken the aspiration.

"Even should the world be engulfed in fire,
Nevertheless pass through it to hear the dharma.
You will encounter the path to become a buddha
And universally save those in the cycle of birth and death."

The Buddha said to Ānanda, "All the bodhisattvas in that land will achieve the stage of becoming a buddha in the next life—except for those who have made an original vow for the sake of sentient beings, pledging to adorn themselves in their virtue, and pursue the deliverance of all sentient beings.

"Ānanda, the śrāvakas in that Buddha land radiate light from their bodies for one fathom, and the light of the bodhisattvas radiates for a hundred yojanas. There are two bodhisattvas who are the most venerable. Their majestic radiant light illuminates throughout the three thousand great thousand realms."

Ānanda asked the Buddha, "What are the names of these two bodhisattvas?"

The Buddha answered, "One is named Avalokiteśvara and the second is named Mahāsthāmaprāpta. These two performed bodhisattva practices in this world, and when their lives came to an end, they were born by transformation in that Buddha's land.

"Ānanda, those sentient beings born in this land all have the thirty-two major marks of a buddha. They are fully possessed of wisdom, delve profoundly into the nature of phenomena, and master the doctrine. Their spiritual powers are unhindered and their sense faculties have keen acuity. Those of lesser acuity obtain the two insights, and those of greater acuity obtain the inestimable insight into the "non-arising" of phenomena. Moreover, the bodhisattvas will attain buddhahood without suffering the unfortunate realms. They will have free command of spiritual powers and knowledge of their past existences, except for those born into other lands of the five corruptions to manifest themselves there as I have in this land."

The Buddha said to Ānanda, "The bodhisattvas in that land, by the spiritual powers of the Buddha, visit all the innumerable realms of the ten directions in the space of a meal and make offerings in homage to all the buddhas, the world honored ones. In accordance with their thoughts, flowers, incense, music, and silk canopies and banners, innumerable and immeasurable materials for offerings, spontaneously transform and appear just as imagined. These are rare and exceptional, and exist not in our world. When given in offering to all the buddhas, bodhisattvas, and the śrāvakas of the assembly, they become suspended in the sky and turn into floral canopies. Their luminescent color, brilliant luster, and fragrance extend everywhere. The circumference of the flowers is four-hundred leagues, which expands in such a way as to extend over the three thousand great thousand realms. As new ones appear one after another, the older ones disappear. The bodhisattvas all rejoice together and, in the sky, perform celestial music of sublime sound. They sing in praise of the Buddha's virtue and listen to the doctrinal teachings, whereby they are immeasurably overjoyed. After making these offerings to the Buddha, even before the next meal, they spontaneously return home to the Land of Bliss."

The Buddha said to Ānanda, "When the Buddha of Infinite Life elucidates the dharma for the śrāvakas and bodhisattvas of the great assembly, they all gather in the lecture hall of seven jewels. The Buddha explains the teaching of the path and relates plainly the wondrous dharma. All rejoice, their minds are liberated, and they achieve the path. Then immediately a breeze spontaneously arises from the four directions, stirring all the jewel trees to emit five tones of melody. Innumerable marvelous flowers rain down and are carried throughout on the wind. Such spontaneously offerings as this are without end. All the myriad celestial deities bring, to the heavens above, one hundred thousand flowers and incense, and ten thousand forms of music in offering to the Buddha and all the bodhisattvas and śrāvakas of the great assembly. They scatter flowers and incense throughout, perform all kinds of music, and one after another make offerings in procession. At which time, the joy of the assembly cannot be captured in words."

The Buddha said to Ānanda, "All the bodhisattvas who live in that Buddha Land, when they lecture it is always the true dharma, and because it is in accord with the wisdom of the Buddha, there is no mistake or omission. In regard to the myriad objects in that land, they have no thought of possession or attachment. Whether to come or go, advance or stop, does not trouble their thoughts, rather they act freely in accordance with their will and do not discriminate in any way. They do not differentiate between self and other, and neither do they compete or argue. Their hearts are filled with great compassion and beneficence towards all sentient beings. Their hearts being magnanimous and imperturbable, they are without anger or enmity. They are pure, separated from worldly desires, and are untiring in their devotions. Their minds are tranquil, valiant, profound, and focused. Furthermore, they are of a mind of adoring the dharma, taking comfort in the dharma, and delighting in the dharma. They have extinguished all the afflictions and parted their minds from the unfortunate destinies. They have mastered all of the bodhisattva practices, and are endowed and accomplished in immeasurable virtues. They achieve profound meditative concentration, spiritual powers, clairvoyance, and transcendent wisdom. They traverse the seven factors of awakening and devote their minds to the Buddha's dharma.

"Their mortal eyes are fine and clear, with nothing they cannot discern; their divine eyes are penetrating, immeasurable and without limit; their dharma eyes are perceptive, comprehending all the paths; their wisdom eyes can see reality transcending to the other shore; they are endowed with the eyes of a buddha by which they awaken to the nature of all things. With this unimpeded wisdom, they expound the dharma for others. They perceive with equanimity that the three realms are empty and non-existent. Intent upon the Buddha's dharma, they acquire the eloquence to eliminate the afflictions suffered by all sentient beings. Arisen from the Tathāgata, the Thus-Come One, they comprehend the reality of all phenomena as is. They know well how to voice the expedient devices of practicing good and extinguishing evil. They do not take joy in mundane discussions, but rejoice in the true discourse.

"Practicing the many roots of good, they are dedicated to and revere the Buddhist path. Knowing that all phenomena, without exception, are unconditioned and quiescent, both their mortal bodies and their afflictions have become extinguished. Hearing the profound dharma, their hearts are free of apprehension and doubt, enabling them to practice constantly. Their great compassion is vast and sublime, encompassing all without discrimination. They have mastered the One Vehicle and transcended to the other shore. Having severed the net of doubt, wisdom springs forth from their hearts to absorb the Buddha's teaching of the dharma completely and without exception.

"Their wisdom is like the vast ocean; their samādhi like the king of mountains. Their wisdom glows in pure radiance, outshining the sun and moon. They are fully endowed with the pristine white dharma. Moreover, they are like the snow-covered Himalayas, because they reflect all the virtues equally and purely. They are like the earth, because they do not distinguish between the pure and sullied, attractive and vile. They are like pure water, because they cleanse the afflictions and all defilements. They are like a raging fire, because they burn away the fuel of the afflictions. They are like a typhoon, because they travel through all the worlds without obstruction. They are like empty space, because they have no place for anything to attach. They are like a lotus flower, because they are unsullied in any realm. They are like the Great Vehicle, because they carry sentient beings out of the cycle of birth and death. They are like thunderclouds, because they rattle the thunder of the great dharma to awaken the unenlightened. They are like a rain-shower, because they shower the nectar of the dharma benefiting all sentient beings. They are like an adamantine mountain, because they cannot be shaken by demons and unbelievers. They are like the king of the Brahma heaven, because they are at the head of all good means. They are like the nyagrodha tree, because they shelter over all. They are like the udumbara blossom, because they are rare and difficult to encounter. They are like a garuḍa bird, because they vanquish false teachings. They are like migratory birds, because they are not possessive or acquisitive. They are like a king of bulls, because they cannot be defeated. They are like a king of elephants, because they pacify all. They are like a king of lions, because they fear of nothing. They are like the broad sky, because their great compassion is fair.

"They have eliminated the feeling of envy, because they do not despise those superior. They joyfully pursue the dharma wholeheartedly with no sense of weariness. They are always desirous of spreading the teaching and untiring in their dedication. They beat the drum of the dharma, raise the flag of the dharma, shine the sun of wisdom, and dispel the darkness of delusion. They practice the six deportments of harmony and always engage in presenting the dharma. They are intrepid in their endeavors, with indefatigable hearts. They are the lamps of the world, with unsurpassable fields of merit. They invariably become masters of the way, impartial without favoritism. Simply taking joy in the True Path, they are completely without elation and anguish. They extract the thorns of desire for the relief of the multitude of beings. Their virtue and wisdom is uncommon and outstanding; there are none who do not revere them. They have extinguished the three hindrances and traverse with the various spiritual powers: the causal power of committing to the Buddhist path, the resultant power of progressing on the Buddhist path, the power of transcendental comprehension, the power of fulfilling the vow for sentient beings, the power of expedient devices for saving sentient beings, the power of constant practice, the power of good conduct, the power of mental concentration, the power of fully-attained wisdom, and the power of hearing the voices of the many sentient beings.

"Furthermore, they possess the powers achieved through generosity, following the precepts, forbearance, endeavor, meditation, and wisdom. They also have the powers of right mindfulness, right visioning, and the various spiritual and clairvoyant powers. Likewise, they have the power of pacification to guide sentient beings. They are fully endowed with all the powers such as these.

"In their bodily hue, marks of a buddha, virtue, eloquence, and discernment, they are without equal in these splendid endowments. They make offerings in homage to innumerable buddhas and are in turn constantly praised by all these buddhas. They have mastered all the bodhisattva pāramitā practices; cultivated the three samādhis of emptiness, non-form, and non-desire; and the samādhis of non-arising and non-ceasing. They have left far behind the stages of the śrāvakas and the pratyekabuddhas. Ānanda, all these bodhisattvas have achieved such immeasurable virtues, of which I have only given you the merest outline. Were I to try to explain in detail, it would be impossible even in a thousand million kalpas."

The Buddha said to Maitreya Bodhisattva, the celestials, mortals, and other beings, "The virtues and wisdom of the śrāvakas and bodhisattvas in the land of the Buddha of Infinite Life cannot be sufficiently praised, and likewise for this land, which is of sublime beatitude and pristine pureness. Why would you not strive for good? Be mindful of the path and it will occur naturally; it has no limits above or below, and extends without bounds. You should each strive in endeavor and exert yourself in this pursuit. Assuredly, should you attain transcendence, and achieve birth in this land of peace and sustenance, you will be diverted from the five unfortunate destinies; the five unfortunate destinies will naturally close, allowing limitless ascent along the Buddhist path. Though easy to achieve birth, there are no mortals there. In that land, there is no digression; one is naturally drawn forward. Why would one not abandon worldly affairs, endeavor in practice, and pursue the path of virtue? One could obtain exceedingly long life and have a life of beatitude without end.

"Yet, people of the mundane realm are superficial in nature and rival each other in their desires. In the midst of tragic misery and extreme suffering, people labor and produce just to get on in the world. Whether respected or reviled, prosperous or impoverished, young or old, male or female, they still worry about their worldly goods. Whether they have or not, they still worry just the same. Turning every which way in anxiety and suffering, they gather woes and build up angst; their hearts are agitated and they are unable to rest at any point. If they own land, they worry about the land; if they own a house, they worry about the house. Likewise, they worry about their horses and oxen and the rest of the six domestic animals, servants, money and wealth, food and clothing, and household furnishings. They accumulate worries and sighs of grief, obsessing in their cares and becoming highly distraught.

"Broadsided by calamities of water and fire, thieves, envious persons, and lenders, their possessions are dissipated and dispersed by being burned, swept away, extorted, or taken. Their anguish becomes a poison causing shudders of fear, with not a moment of release. This angst becomes attached inside their hearts, and they cannot sever their distress and apprehension. Their hearts and minds become hardened, so that they cannot even make a change for the better. Moreover, if they are struck by disaster, their body fails, or when their life comes to an end, they leave all behind and none can they bring with them. Even though exalted or wealthy, they still have this malady. Because of all these fears and anguish, their hardship and suffering is such as this, and all these chills and fevers of distress join together to torment them.

"The poor, low, and needy are already without. Not having fields, they still worry, and desire to have fields. Not having homes, they still worry, and desire to have homes. Not having horses and oxen and the rest of the six domestic animals, servants, money and wealth, food and clothing, and household furnishings, they still worry, and desire to have them. Should they have some, others are lacking, or what they have, it is still too little, and they wish it were as they desired. Even if they get what they desire, it soon vanishes. In this way, they worry and suffer, pursuing their desires, never to be able to attain them. No matter how they plan, they still fail to meet with success. They become exhausted in body and mind, and cannot be at peace whether seated or standing. Because of these worries and cares, their hardship and suffering is such as this, and all these chills and fevers of distress join together to torment them. At some point due to this, their bodies are exhausted and their life cut short. They are unable to do good, follow the path, or accumulate merit. When their life ends, their body dies, and they must go off alone into the distance. Although there is room for choosing their destiny, the paths of good and evil, none of them are able to apprehend it."

"People of the mundane realm, parent and child, older and younger sibling, husband and wife, close and distant relatives, should all have love and respect for each other, and not hatred and bitterness. Whether they have or have not, they should sympathize with each other and not be covetous or be parsimonious. They should accommodate by word and facial expression and not act against each other's wishes. However, if at times, they are of a mind of altercation and become wrathful, the enmity in this life, mutually held in subtleties of hatred and bitterness, will then in their following lives transform dramatically until becoming deep seated resentment.

"Why would this be? In the matters of the mundane world, there is mutual injury and scarring. Although the harm to each other may not be immediate or at once, nevertheless loaded with venom, laden with anger, with fury attached to the psyche, naturally it becomes inscribed permanently in the heart, and neither side can disengage. They will be reborn into the world together and once again retaliate against each other.

"While people exist within the mundane world of desire, they are born alone, die alone, depart alone, and return alone. Their previous conduct affects their destiny, whether it is a state of peace or suffering. This must be done by they themselves and no one can take their place. Good or evil conduct transforms to misfortune or prosperity, the future states of which strictly await them, and this destiny they must enter alone. They reach a far different place, that no one can see. Their birth in such a place naturally is according to good or evil conduct. The separation to the dark and faint reaches will be long lasting. If the road taken is not the same, there will be no chance of meeting, and it will be very, very difficult to reunite.

"Why would you not discard these worldly matters, and while still strong and vital, exert yourself in practicing good and endeavor in aspiration for transcendence to the other world? What an extremely long life you could attain! Why would you not pursue the Buddhist path? Why would you dawdle at ease and what pleasure would you hope to find?"

"Such are the people of this mundane world that they do not believe in practicing good to attain good, or following the path to attain the path. They do not believe that when people die, they will be reborn, and that charity and giving begets merit. They have complete disbelief in the matter of good and evil, thinking it to be unnatural and that in the end there is no such thing. Still yet, for this very reason, they themselves see this as correct.

"Furthermore, upon observing each other, those before and after become likewise. Still more is this influence passed on, with the parents perpetuating it. Parents and grandparents from the outset do not practice good, and do not know the virtue of the path. They are foolish in body and their spirit dark; their hearts are choked and their minds closed. The destiny of the cycle of birth and death and the paths of good and evil, they themselves cannot see and have no one to tell them. Auspicious and inauspicious, fortune and misfortune, each alternate in occurrence, with none suspecting the cause.

"The way of birth and death is constant, repeated over and over. The parent mourns for the child, the child mourns for the parent, brothers and sisters, and husbands and wives mourn for each other. This reversal of the proper order is the basis of impermanence. All must pass to the beyond; none can remain forever. Although the teaching is described to open the path, there are few who believe. This is why the cycle of birth and death continues without cease.

"People such as this are deluded with false views, and do not believe in the doctrine of the dharma. They are mindless of the distant future and only pursue their desires. They are led astray by their passion and desire, so that they cannot reach the path of virtue. They fall astray by their anger and become avaricious for wealth and sensual pleasure. Because of this, they cannot attain the path. Moreover, they will again suffer the unfortunate destinies, and their cycle of birth and death will repeat without end. How pitiful and wretched!

"There are times when, in a family of parent and child, brothers and sisters, and husband and wife, that one dies while yet one still lives. They are left to grieve together, yearning with love and appreciation. They are bound with grief, suffer emotionally, and continue together in longing. Even as the days pass and they age, they do not overcome it. Although the teaching of the path of virtue is described, their hearts are not opened to the light. Dwelling on love and affection, they cannot sever their thoughts of passion and desire. They are closed in darkness obscuring their reason and wrapped in delusion. They cannot think or cogitate deeply, make their minds upright, dedicate themselves to endeavoring on the path, or divorce themselves from worldly matters. They are at a loss until the end, and when at the end of their life they still were not able to attain the path, then there is nothing they can do.

"Defiled and indulgent, all crave love and desire. Those who have strayed from the path are many, and those who have realized it are few. They are engrossed in worldly matters, where nothing can be relied on. Exalted or humble, lofty or lowly, wealthy or poor, lofty or base, they are preoccupied with hardship and suffering, each harboring murderous venom. This evil intent shadows them in darkness, so that they become enthralled in such unconscionable matters. They upset the law of heaven and earth, and do not concede to human feeling. They naturally do evil and wrong, first acceding to it, then willfully excusing their own acts, awaiting the ends of their offenses. Even though their life has not yet reached its term, already is it lost at once. They fall into the unfortunate paths, to suffer hardship in succeeding lifetimes. There they repeat the cycle of rebirth for some hundred billion of aeons, with no chance of escape. Their pain is indescribable. How grievous indeed!"

The Buddha said to Maitreya Bodhisattva, the celestial deities, humans, and other beings, "Now I have told you the condition of the mundane world. Mortals, for this reason, cannot attain the path. You must seriously weigh your thoughts and distance yourself from all evil. Choose that which is good and exert yourself in practicing it. Love and desire, splendor and prosperity cannot last forever; all will be parted from one and cannot be savored. While I, the Buddha, am in this world, you should exert yourself in this endeavor. By sincerely aspiring to be born in the Land of Serenity and Beatitude, you can attain pervasive clarity in wisdom and extreme merit. Do not accede to your heart's desires, disregard the Buddhist precepts, or fall behind others. Should you have questions, or do not understand the scripture, you can ask for details from me the Buddha, whereby I will explain."

Maitreya Bodhisattva knelt down in a bow and said, "The Buddha is almighty and venerable, what you have expounded is pleasing and good. Listening to the Buddha's words of the doctrine, my heart was touched and I thought, the people of the mundane realm are truly like that, just as the Buddha said. Now the Buddha, with vast compassion, has revealed the great path. Our eyes and ears have been opened to the light and at last we can attain deliverance. Upon hearing the Buddha's expounding, there was no one who was not overjoyed.

"From the celestial deities to humans and even species that crawl on the ground, all received this great mercy and emancipation from grief and suffering. The Buddha's words of teaching and counsel are supremely profound and good. The radiance of your wisdom is seen from the eight directions, above and below, and the past, future, and present; it cannot but be thorough and penetrating. That I and the entire assembly have now received the attainment of liberation is all due to the Buddha, who in prior lifetimes sought the path in stringent endeavor. Your compassionate nature is universally embracing, your merit high and lofty, and your radiant light permeating and illuminating, extending infinitely into the void. You open the gate to nirvana, bestow the doctrine and induce its understanding, eliminate false conduct, shaking the ten directions without end or limit. The Buddha is the lord of the dharma and your excellence surpasses that of all the venerable ones. You are the instructor of all celestials and mortals universally, so that they all can, according to their inclinations and aspirations, attain the path. Now having had this chance to encounter the Buddha and hear the name of the Buddha of Infinite Life, there were none who were not overjoyed and their hearts opened to the light."

The Buddha said to Maitreya Bodhisattva, "What you say is so. Should there be those who revere the compassion of the Buddha, they would truly gain great virtue. It will be a long, long time until there is again a Buddha below the heavens. Now, when I was in this realm and became a buddha, I expounded the scriptural dharma, transmitted the teaching of the path, severed the nets of doubt, removed the roots of desire, closed the source of the many evils, and traversed the three realms freely. The wisdom of the scriptural texts is the basis of all the Buddhist paths, and grasping its line will illuminate and clarify. It will reveal the five destinies, and those not yet delivered will be delivered. It will resolve the truth of birth and death, and the path of nirvana.

"Maitreya, you must know this, since over innumerable aeons you have practiced the bodhisattva conduct wishing to deliver sentient beings from long ago. Following you to attain the path and then reach nirvana were those in numbers that cannot be recounted. You and the celestial deities, humans, and the four groups of adherents of the ten directions have over many aeons revolved in the five paths of existence with indescribable misery and suffering. Still in the present world, the cycle of birth and death has not ceased, but now you have encountered the Buddha, heard the scriptural dharma, and moreover been able to hear the Buddha of Infinite Life. How pleasing and extremely fortunate, that I can share this joy with you.

"Furthermore, you should now abhor the pain and suffering of birth, death, old age, and sickness. The veils of evil are impure and not to be savored. It is appropriate to sever yourself from them, be upright in form, proper in conduct, and increase the practice of good. You should purify yourself for practice and cleanse the impurities of your mind so that your deeds are true to your word and your inner thoughts and outward expression match. People should attain transcendence themselves and also turn to save others. They should endeavor in their vow to save others and accumulate the roots of good.

"Even if you struggle and suffer for the brief period of one lifetime, soon you will be born in the land of the Buddha of Infinite Life. There you will have limitless ease, at length receive the result of the path of virtue, sever the roots of the cycle of birth and death, and not again suffer the maladies of avarice, enmity, and delusion. Should you wish for a lifespan of one aeon, a hundred aeons, or even a quadrillion aeons, you need only to think of it and you can attain it. The unconditioned nature of that land is next to the path of nirvana. You and the others should make every effort to pursue your aspiration. You must not acquire doubts and despair midway, nor make offenses, otherwise you will be born in a seven-jewel pavilion at the border-region, and for the five hundred years of your life there, you will incur various misfortunes."

Maitreya said to the Buddha, "Having received the Buddha's venerable teaching, I will devote myself to its practice and study, perform conduct according to the teaching, and never engage in doubt."

The Buddha said to Maitreya, "Should you and others be able in this world to be upright in mind and correct in thought, and not practice any of the host of evils, then this would indeed be the utmost virtue. In the worlds of the ten directions, this is without compare. Why is this? In the many buddha lands, the groups of celestial deities and humans naturally perform good and do not commit any great evil; it is easy for them to be edified. Now I have become a buddha in this world, a place of the five evils, the five resultant pains, and the five burnings, which makes it extremely difficult. I instruct and transform the many living beings, enabling them to discard the five evils, part from the five pains, and withdraw from the five burnings. I subdue and transform their thoughts, enabling them to maintain the five good acts, acquire merit and virtue, transcendence of this world, longevity, and the path of nirvana."

The Buddha said, "What are these five evils, five pains, and five burnings? How do you eliminate the five evils, maintain the good acts, acquire merit and virtue, transcendence of this world, longevity, and the path of nirvana?"

The Buddha said, "This is the first evil. The celestials, humans, and even species that crawl on the ground like to commit a host of evils. There are none who are otherwise. The strong oppress the weak. They turn upon each other inflicting harm. They cause murder and injury, biting and devouring each other. They do not know how to practice good, are grievous in their evil, and without the path, and afterwards they incur the retribution that is their natural destiny. The celestial luminaries keep conscientious records and do not pardon their transgressions. For that reason, there are those who suffer poverty, lowly stature, begging for food, abandonment, deafness, muteness, and blindness, delusion, perversity, in addition to conditions of hunchback, madness, and idiocy. There are also those who have nobility, wealth, talent, and brilliance, because they all were in previous lives filial and compassionate, practiced good, and accumulated virtue.

"In the mundane world, it is the customary way to have the king's law and incarceration. They who have no sense of trepidation and prudence, commit offenses leading to punishment, and incur their retribution. Even should one hope to be liberated, it is difficult to attain pardon and be released. This is the circumstances of the mundane world seen right before the eyes. When life ends, the afterworld is extremely deep and relentless. Entering such dark and dismal realm, one is transferred to the next life and receives a body, and as in the case of the king's law, suffers extreme punishment.

"For this reason, they will naturally incur the immeasurable pain and suffering of the three realms of defilement, which will be transferred to their person and their form adapted to the ordained path. At which, they attain life, which may be long or short, and their spirit and consciousness is naturally destined to this. One must face this alone, only to be born together with one's adversary, to once again retaliate against each other without end. Until this evil karma has been exhausted, they cannot separate from each other. While in this cycle, they cannot leave at any time. It is difficult to attain release and their pain is indescribable. Everywhere between heaven and earth, this is natural. Although the response may not be immediate or at once, according to the path of good or evil, it will return to meet them.

"This is the first great evil, the first pain, the first burning. The pain and suffering is such as this, for instance like a great fire burning a person's body. Should people be able amidst this to wholeheartedly set their minds, be upright in form and proper in conduct, solely do good, and not practice any of the host of evils, then those people alone will be liberated, acquire merit and virtue, transcendence of this world, ascent to the Pure Land above, and the path of nirvana. This is the first great good."

The Buddha said, "This is the second evil. People of the mundane world, parent and child, older and younger sibling, family members, husband and wife, they are all irresponsible and do not obey the law. Extravagant and wanton, arrogant and selfish, they desire all the pleasures. They give themselves up to their feelings and self-indulgence, and moreover deceive and fool each other. Their mind and mouth each differ and their speech and motives are not true. Their flattery and obsequiousness is insincere, using clever speech to curry favor. They are jealous of the wise and slander the good, and entrap them with false charges.

"When the ruler is not perceptive and relies on the ministers, the ministers busy themselves with weaving deceit. They trample the law to accomplish their affairs, aware of the opportunities. When the ruler does not reign properly, he is deceived and loyalty and devotion to him is heedlessly lost. The will of heaven is contravened. The minister deceives the lord, the child deceives the parent. Older and younger siblings, husbands and wives, close and distant friends, all deceive and betray each other. Each embraces avarice, enmity, and delusion; profusely desiring only for themselves, and greedily desiring in plenty. The exalted and humble, lofty and lowly, are all naturally alike at heart.

"Their home destroyed, their life lost, they do not look fore and aft, and both near and distant relatives are ruined by this. There are times when members of the same groups whether family, scholars, villagers, townspeople, unlettered commoners, or rustics could turn to each other under such circumstances, but even then they cause one another harm for the sake of gain, and become angered and entangled in enmity. If they have any wealth, they become parsimonious and are not in the least generous. They love their treasures and it weighs on them to be poor. Their hearts are labored and their body suffers. In this way they reach the end, and have nothing left to rely on. Alone they have arrived and alone they will depart, with no one to accompany them. The cause of good or bad, and the affect of good or ill fortune, will direct them to the fate of their next birth, determining whether it will be a place of ease, or they will fall into one of hardship and suffering. Naturally afterwards, they feel remorse, but what could they then do?

"People of the mundane world, their minds are deluded and their wisdom lacking. Seeing the good, they despise and defame it and do not think to yearn after it. They only wish to do evil, and heedlessly do they go against the law. Always harboring hearts of avarice, they covet the gain of others, which they waste and squander only to again seek out more. They with hearts of iniquity, who are unrighteous, cringe before the countenance of others. They do not foresee that this situation will lead to remorse, but indeed it does.

"In this world there appears the king's law and incarceration, where one's fate is according to the offense, and punishment is incurred. The cause of this is from a former life, when the virtue of the path was not believed and the roots of good not practiced. Should now evil be repeated, the celestial deities will engrave it, registering each name individually. When their life ends, and their spirit departs, they will fall into the unfortunate paths. For this reason, they will naturally incur the immeasurable pain and suffering of the three realms of defilement. They will repeat the cycle of rebirth for aeons of succeeding lifetimes, without any time of leave, and it will be difficult to attain release. Their pain cannot be expressed.

"This is the second great evil, the second pain, the second burning. The pain and suffering is such as this, for instance like a great fire burning a person's body. Should people be able amidst this to wholeheartedly set their minds, be upright in form and proper in conduct, solely do good, and not practice any of the host of evils, then those people alone will be liberated, acquire merit and virtue, transcendence of this world, ascent to the Pure Land above, and the path of nirvana. This is the second great good."

The Buddha said, "This is the third evil. People of the mundane world are born relying on each other and live together between heaven and earth. The years of one's life cannot be estimated. Among the upper level are those with wisdom, dignity, nobility, and wealth, and among the lower level are the poor, ignoble, feeble, and foolish. Within this are those people without good, who are habitually attached to evil and have only licentious thoughts, filling their breast with anguish. They are disturbed by love and desire and cannot rest whether seated or standing.

"They bind their object of desire, in a vain attempt to get what they want. They gaze lewdly at those with delicate complexions, until their indecent thoughts are externalized. They despise their wives, and recklessly have affairs. Their household possessions are lost, and they do things against the law. They band together to form groups, skirmish, and attack each other. They go against the path by assaulting, threatening, murdering, and plundering. Their evil thoughts become overt and they no longer exert themselves in their endeavors.

"They attain a trifling through theft, and become bound by desire to do more. They frighten and bully to provide for their wives and children. They do as their hearts desire and make themselves extremely comfortable. Moreover, as regards to their family, whether exalted or humble, the household and distant relatives are all caused pain and suffering by this. Furthermore, they have no fear of the sanctions of the king's law.

"Such evils as these become evident among humans and spirits. Brought to light by the sun and moon, they are seen by the gods and deities who make conscientious records. For this reason, they will naturally incur the immeasurable pain and suffering of the three realms of defilement. They will repeat the cycle of rebirth for aeons of succeeding lifetimes, without any time of leave, and it will be difficult to attain release. Their pain cannot be expressed.

"This is the third great evil, the third pain, the third burning. The pain and suffering is such as this, for instance like a great fire burning a person's body. Should people be able amidst this to wholeheartedly set their minds, be upright in form and proper in conduct, solely do good, and not practice any of the host of evils, then those people alone will be liberated, acquire merit and virtue, transcendence of this world, ascent to the Pure Land above, and the path of nirvana. This is the third great good."

The Buddha said, "This is the fourth evil. People of the mundane world are not mindful of practicing good. They incite each other to carry out together a host of evils. They are two-tongued, bad-mouthed, reckless in their remarks, and fanciful in speech. They disparage others and cause contention, hate and envy good people, and ruin the sensible, at which they remain self-complacent. They are not filial to their parents, fail to respect their teachers and elders, are not trusted by their friends, and find it difficult to be genuine. They think most highly of themselves and ascribe to their own logic. They throw their weight around and look down on others. They have no self-awareness and commit evil without shame. They consider themselves strong and robust, and expect others to prostrate themselves in fear. They are not awed by heaven and earth, the gods and deities, or the sun and moon. They do not practice any good whatsoever and are difficult to subdue. They allow their own faults and lameness as reasonable, have no sense of trepidation, and accept their own arrogance as normal.

"Their many evils such as this are conscientiously recorded by the celestial deities. Though they may rely on the vast merit and virtue made in previous lives, and their few past good deeds would serve to aid them, the evil they have done in the present life will extinguish that merit and virtue. All the virtuous spirits and gods will withdraw from them and they will be left alone standing in the void, with nowhere to turn for support. When their life ends, all their accumulated evil acts will come back to them and naturally they will be compelled by this to meet their fate.

"Moreover, their name will be registered, and the gods and deities will remember it. Their offenses will draw them to their fate. Naturally, they will be unable to evade the punishment of their offenses. Rather, as a result of their previous conduct, they will be burned in a fiery cauldron, broken in body and mind, and their spirit will be subjected to pain and suffering. If at such time, they feel remorse, what could they then do? Naturally the way of heaven will not falter.

"For this reason, they will naturally incur the immeasurable pain and suffering of the three realms of defilement. They will repeat the cycle of rebirth for aeons of succeeding lifetimes, without any time of leave, and it will be difficult to attain release. Their pain cannot be expressed.

"This is the fourth great evil, the fourth pain, the fourth burning. The pain and suffering is such as this, for instance like a great fire burning a person's body. Should people be able amidst this to wholeheartedly set their minds, be upright in form and proper in conduct, solely do good, and not practice any of the host of evils, then those people alone will be liberated, acquire merit and virtue, transcendence of this world, ascent to the Pure Land above, and the path of nirvana. This is the fourth great good."

The Buddha said, "This is the fifth evil. People of the mundane world are slothful and indolent. They do not practice any good whatsoever and shirk in their endeavors, so their household and dependents suffer from hunger and cold. When exhorted to mend their ways by their mother and father, their eyes bulge in anger. They ignore what they are told and are defiant and insubordinate, so that it is like a home of hostility and their parents do not recognize their child. They take without regard to propriety, and become repugnant and loathsome to people at large. They lack a sense of obligation, disregard their responsibilities, and feel no need to make recompense. They will become poor and destitute, and unable to be restored.

"They plunder and appropriate the possessions of others, and then squander it away. It becomes habit for them to repeatedly gain by these means, which they use to satisfy their appetites. They indulge in wine and feast on delicacies, eating and drinking without limit. They do as their hearts desire and become profligate. They are foolish by nature and quarrelsome. They are insensitive to other's feelings, and wish to force their will on them. When they see people who are good, they loathe them with hatred and envy. They have no sense of responsibility or respect, nor reflect on their conduct. They are self-complacent in their arrogance and cannot be admonished.

"They have no concern whether their six filial relations and dependents have the necessities or not. They do not consider their obligation to their fathers and mothers, nor their responsibilities to their friends and superiors. Their hearts are always set on evil thoughts, their mouths on evil words, their bodies on evil conduct, without a single good. They do not believe in the ancient sages nor the scriptural dharma of the buddhas. They do not believe that in following the path one can attain transcendence to the other world. They do not believe that after death, their spirit will be reborn. They do not believe that doing good begets good, and doing evil begets evil. They are willing to kill an arhat and destroy the harmony of the Buddhist community. They are willing to injure their parents, siblings, and dependents. Their six filial relations loathe them and wish for their death.

"Such as this are the people of the mundane world, all of the same mind and intention. Deluded and blind, even using what wisdom they may have, they do not know whence they came before birth, nor their destiny after death. They have neither a sense of benevolence, nor of the proper order of things, and wickedly defy heaven and earth. In spite of this, they hope for happy circumstances and wish for long life, but death must come to meet them. Those with compassionate feelings instruct and exhort them that they may contemplate good, and disclose that in the cycle of life and death the fate of good and evil is such by nature, but they do not believe it. Regardless of pains taken to explain, it has no effect on them. Their hearts are shut closed and their minds are not open to understanding.

"When the end of their life is imminent, they feel remorse and fear in succession. Not having practiced good, just when confronted with the end do they feel remorse, but what use is it to feel remorse afterwards? The five paths of existence between heaven and earth become manifest, stretching broad and deep, vast and wide. According to good and evil, does fortune and disaster follow, which must be borne by oneself and no one can take their place.

"Such is the principle of nature, that according to what they practice, their offenses will pursue them throughout their life, and cannot be rid of. Good people do good, and go from happiness into happiness, from light into light. Evil people do evil, and go from suffering into suffering, dark into dark. Who is able to know this? It is only the Buddha, who explains the teaching and discloses it, but there are few who believe. Birth and death continue without rest, and there is no cessation of the unfortunate paths. Such are the people of the mundane world that it is difficult to express in particulars.

"For this reason, they will naturally incur the immeasurable pain and suffering of the three realms of defilement. They will repeat the cycle of rebirth for aeons of succeeding lifetimes, without any time of leave, and it will be difficult to attain release. Their pain cannot be expressed.

"This is the fifth great evil, the fifth pain, the fifth burning. The pain and suffering is such as this, for instance like a great fire burning a person's body. Should people be able amidst this to wholeheartedly set their minds, be upright in form and proper in thought, their words and actions correspond, their deeds sincere, their speech and words in accord, their hearts and mouth not differ, solely do good, and not practice any of the host of evils, then those people alone will be liberated, acquire merit and virtue, transcendence of this world, ascent to the Pure Land above, and the path of nirvana. This is the fifth great good."

The Buddha said to Maitreya, "I have just explained to you and the others how the five evils of this world cause pain and suffering. The five pains and five burnings will arise again repeatedly. Those who only do evil and do not practice the roots of good will all naturally enter the unfortunate destinies, and in this world they will be inflicted with incurable ills so that they may wish for death but not attain it, or wish to live but not attain it. These evil effects they incur will become apparent and seen by all. When their body dies, according to their conduct they will enter the three unfortunate paths and suffer immeasurable pain and torment, where they will burn in a fire of their own creation.

"For a long time after, they form mutual bonds of enmity progressing from causing minor incidences to doing great evil. They all lust after material goods and objects of carnal desire, and are incapable of charity. They are driven by the foolishness of desire with these thoughts attached to their heart. They are bound by the afflictions with no possibility of release. They contend ardently for their own benefit, with no reflecting back. Only when they have wealth and prosperity are they content. They are unable to practice forbearance or endeavor in performing good. Their strength is not unlimited and they will grind to exhaustion. Their body is set in pain and suffering, and for long after do they suffer great strife.

"The way of heaven stretches far and wide, naturally apprehending each and every deed in its meshes, large and small, without regard to high or low. Caught in this, they are disconsolate and distraught. Such has it been from the past to the present. How painful and piteous!"

The Buddha said to Maitreya, "The mundane world is like this, and the buddhas all lament it. By their majestic spiritual power are the host of evils destroyed, enabling all and every good be done: the abandonment of disruptive thought, the maintaining of the doctrine and precepts, progress on the path of the dharma, with no false step or shortcoming made, and in the end the attainment of transcendence of this world and the path of nirvana."

The Buddha said, "You and all the celestials and humans of the present, as well as people of the latter worlds, having attained the scriptural words of the Buddha, you should consider them in earnest, so you may in the midst of this be upright in mind and proper in conduct. Those superior do good and edify those below. Transmit the instruction from one to another and maintain each aspect to its foundation! Honor the sages and revere the good, have benevolent mercy and all-encompassing compassion. Do not in the least ignore or oppose the teachings and admonitions of the Buddha. You should seek transcendence of this world, eradicate the many evil roots of the cycle of birth and death, and part from the three realms of defilement, the path of immeasurable despair, terror, and pain and suffering.

"Should you and the others while here plant the roots of virtue widely, spread your compassion and extend your generosity, and not violate the proscriptions of the Buddhist path; should you practice forbearance, devotional practices, single-minded dedication, and wisdom; should you transmit the dharma for mutual edification, and practice virtue and establish good; should you maintain proper thoughts and proper intentions, keep the precepts of abstinence, and purify yourself, for a day and a night, then this would be superior to practicing good for a hundred years in the Land of Infinite Life. Why is this? That buddha land is one of unconditioned nature where all accumulate much good and there is not one hair of evil.

"Should you, while here, practice good for ten days and ten nights, then that would be superior to practicing good for a thousand years in the buddha worlds of the other directions. Why is this? In the buddha worlds of the other directions, those who do good are many, and those who do evil are few. Merit and virtue are naturally occurring, and no evil is made in that land.

"However, in this world are evils many, and without such natural benefits, there is the pain and suffering of yearning and desire, mutual falsehood and deceit, and physical and mental anguish. They imbibe pain and dine on bitterness. In this way, they are pressed by worldly affairs, without even a breath of respite.

"Out of compassion for you and the groups of celestial deities and humans, do I painstakingly teach and guide you so that you may practice good. According to your capacity has the path been opened and the scriptural dharma bestowed, without exception, so all may attain the path in accord with the aspirations held in your mind.

"Wherever the Buddha traverses, kingdom or province, village or hamlet, there are none who are not transformed. All below heaven will be in harmony and order. The sun and moon will be clear and bright, the wind and rain will be in season, and no disaster or plague will occur. The kingdom will flourish and the people will be at peace, and there will be no need for arms. They will esteem virtue, foster benevolence, and diligently practice propriety and humility."

The Buddha said, "I feel compassion and sympathy for you and the celestial deities and humans, beyond what a father and mother feels for their child. Now that I have become a Buddha in this world, I have subjugated the five evils, eliminated the five pains, extinguished the five burnings, countered evil with good, and removed the suffering of birth and death, so that you may acquire the five virtues and ascendance to unconditioned beatitude. After I have passed from this world, the path of my scripture will gradually become extinct and people will be subject to flattery and deception, and again commit a host of evils. The five burnings and five pains will recur as before the dharma. For long afterwards will this continue in increasing severity. As it cannot be explained thoroughly, I have but described it in brief for you."

The Buddha said to Maitreya, "All of you should each think well on this. You should transmit the teaching and exhort each other, keep in accordance with the scriptural dharma of the Buddha, and not go contrary to it."

At which, Maitreya Bodhisattva clasped hands together and said, "As the Buddha has so painstakingly expounded, the people of the mundane world are really so. The Tathāgata has universal compassion and sympathy, comprehensively enabling transcendence. Having received the Buddha's repeated instruction, we will uphold it with no false step or shortcoming made."

The Buddha said to Ānanda, "Rise, rearrange your robes, put your palms together in respect, and revere the Buddha of Infinite Life. All the buddhas, the tathāgatas from the lands of the ten directions constantly raise their voices in unison to praise that Buddha, who is unattached and unimpeded."

At this, Ānanda rose, rearranged his robes, straightened his posture, and faced the west. In reverence, he placed his palms together and prostrated his entire body to the ground paying homage to the Buddha of Infinite Life. Then he said, "World Honored One, I wish to see that Buddha, the Land of Serenity and Beatitude, along with all the bodhisattvas, śrāvakas, and the great assembly."

As soon as Ānanda had said this, immediately the Buddha of Infinite Life emitted a great radiant light that universally illuminated the entirety of all the buddha worlds. The Encircling Adamantine Mountain, the King of Mountains Sumeru, the great and smaller mountains—everywhere was all basked in the same color. It was just as a cosmic flood at the end of the world, in which all myriad things are submerged and indiscernible, and only a vast expanse of a great body of overflowing water could be seen. Moreover, that Buddha's radiant light was such that all the radiant light of the śrāvakas and bodhisattvas was utterly obscured, and only the brilliance and radiance of the Buddha's light could be seen.

At that moment, Ānanda immediately saw the Buddha of Infinite Life, as majestic and lofty as the King of Mountains Sumeru, raising high above all the worlds. There was nowhere not illuminated by the radiant light of the Buddha's marks. The four groups of adherents gathered in the assembly all saw it at once, and those in that land likewise saw this land in the same manner.

At that time, the Buddha said to Ānanda and the Bodhisattva Merciful One, "You have seen that Buddha's land, but did you see it from the ground up to the Pure Abode Heaven, and within it all the objects that are naturally sublime and gloriously pure?"

Ānanda responded, "Yes, I certainly saw it."

"Then did you also hear the Buddha of Infinite Life's great voice extending throughout all the worlds to transform sentient beings?"

Ānanda responded, "Yes, I certainly heard it."

"The people of that land ride on seven-jewel palaces of a hundred thousand yojanas reaching without hindrance the ten directions to make offerings to all the buddhas. Did you see this as well?"

Ānanda responded, "I saw it."

"The people of that realm who are born of womb, did you also see this?"

Ānanda responded, "I saw it."

"Those born of womb reside in palaces of one hundred yojanas or five hundred yojanas. There inside, each enjoys all the various pleasures, just as the Heaven of the Thirty-Three Celestials is everything naturally conditioned."

At that time, the bodhisattva Merciful One addressed the Buddha and said, "World Honored One, what are the causes and conditions by which people of that land are born in the womb or born by transformation?"

The Buddha replied to the Merciful One, "Should there be sentient beings who, while harboring doubts in their mind, practice meritorious virtue aspiring to be born in that land, they do not grasp the Buddha Wisdom, the Unconceivable Wisdom, the Ineffable Wisdom, the Great-Vehicle of Vast Wisdom, and the Peerless Unsurpassed Supreme Excellent Wisdom. In regard to each of these wisdoms, they have doubts and lack faith. Yet do they believe in retribution and merit, cultivate the roots of good, and aspire to be born in that land. It is these sentient beings who are born in those palaces, with a lifespan of five-hundred years, where never can they see the Buddha, nor hear the doctrine of the dharma, nor see the bodhisattvas, śrāvakas, and the sages of the assembly. For that reason, these of that land are said to be born of womb."

"Should there be sentient beings who clearly believe in the Buddha Wisdom through the Excellent Wisdom, who produce merit and transfer it in sincere belief, then these sentient beings will naturally be born by transformation seated cross-legged in a seven-jewel blossom. In a matter of an instant, they will have the bodily marks, radiant light, wisdom, and virtue, just as the bodhisattvas who are so endowed and made perfect.

"In addition, Merciful One, if the great bodhisattvas from the buddha lands of other directions awaken the desire to see the Buddha of Infinite Life, pay homage and make offerings to the Buddha and to the assembly of bodhisattvas and śrāvakas, then these bodhisattvas will, when their life ends, attain birth in the Land of Infinite Life and will naturally be born by transformation in a seven-jewel blossom.

"Maitreya, you should know that the reason for those being born by transformation is their exceptional wisdom. Whereas, all those born of womb are lacking wisdom. During their five hundred years of life, they will never see that Buddha, nor hear the scriptural dharma, nor see the assembly of bodhisattvas and śrāvakas, nor have the means to make offerings to the buddhas, nor know the observances of the bodhisattvas, nor be able to practice virtue. You should know that it is because these beings, while they lodged in this world, did not have wisdom and harbored doubts."

The Buddha said to Maitreya, "Should, for example, a Cakravartin King have a separate palace chamber of seven jewels, variously adorned with cushions laid and curtains hung, and if there were some young princes who made offenses against the king and were confined in this palace tied with gold chains, but were provided with food and drink, clothing, cushions, flowers and perfumes, and entertainments, just as the Cakravartin King himself with nothing lacking, what do you think? Would these princes enjoy this place, or not?"

Maitreya answered, "No, indeed not. On the contrary, by all means, appealing to those with great power, they would wish to free themselves."

The Buddha said to Maitreya, "These sentient beings are also likewise.

Due to doubting the buddha wisdoms, they are born in those palatial chambers. There is no punishment, nor even a single instance of ill treatment. However, for five hundred years, they will not see the three treasures, nor will they be able to make offerings and cultivate the roots of good. For this reason, they will suffer. Although they have other pleasures, they still do not enjoy this place. If these sentient beings were to discern this root of their offense, feel deep remorse and seek removal from this place, then immediately upon having this thought, they would be conveyed to the place of the Buddha of Infinite Life, where they could pay homage and make offerings. They could also reach the places of immeasurable, innumerable buddhas, and there practice meritorious virtue. Maitreya, you should know that even bodhisattvas who give rise to doubts will lose these great benefits. For this reason, you must clearly believe in the unsurpassed wisdom of the buddhas."

Maitreya Bodhisattva said to the Buddha, "World Honored One, how many bodhisattvas of the stage of non-retrogression from this world are born in that Buddha's land?" The Buddha responded to Maitreya, "In this world, there are six billion and seven hundred million bodhisattvas of the stage of non-retrogression who achieve birth in that land. Each bodhisattva has already made offerings to innumerable buddhas, following just after you Maitreya. Even those bodhisattvas who have yet done little conduct or performed but few virtuous practices, who are of incalculable numbers, will all achieve birth."

The Buddha said to Maitreya, "It is not just the bodhisattvas of my realm who achieve birth in that Buddha's land; it is also the same for the buddha lands of the other directions. The first of these buddhas is called Far Shining, and the eighteen billion bodhisattvas there will all achieve birth. The second of these buddhas is called Treasure House, and the nine billion bodhisattvas there will all achieve birth. The third of these buddhas is called Immeasurable Sound, and the twenty-two billion bodhisattvas there will all achieve birth. The fourth of these buddhas is called Ambrosia Flavor, and the twenty-five billion bodhisattvas there will all achieve birth. The fifth of these buddhas is called Dragon Slayer, and the one billion and four hundred million bodhisattvas there will all achieve birth. The sixth of these buddhas is called Victorious Power, and the fourteen thousand bodhisattvas there will all achieve birth. The seventh of these buddhas is called Lion, and the fifty billion bodhisattvas there will all achieve birth. The eighth of these buddhas is called Undefiled Light, and the eight billion bodhisattvas there will all achieve birth. The ninth of these buddhas is called Virtue Leader, and the six billion bodhisattvas there will all achieve birth. The tenth of these buddhas is called Mount of Marvelous-Virtue, and the six billion bodhisattvas there will all achieve birth. The eleventh of these buddhas is called Lord of Men, and the one billion bodhisattvas there will all achieve birth. The twelfth of these buddhas is called Unsurpassed Blossom, and the assembly of innumerable, incalculable bodhisattvas there are all of the stage of non-retrogression, with dauntless wisdom. They have already made offerings to immeasurable numbers of buddhas, and in a mere seven days, have accomplished the great bodhisattva stage of Immutable Dharma, normally only accomplished after practicing for ten trillion of aeons. These bodhisattvas will all achieve birth. The thirteenth of these buddhas is called Fearless, and the assembly of seventy-nine billion great bodhisattvas there, along with the lesser bodhisattvas and the monks of incalculable numbers, will all achieve birth."

The Buddha said to Maitreya, "It is not just the bodhisattvas and other beings of these fourteen buddha lands who will achieve birth, those of immeasurable buddhas lands in the realms of the ten directions will also achieve birth in this way in great uncountable numbers, but for me to explain the names of these buddhas of the ten directions, and the bodhisattvas and monks to be born in that land, would take day and night for an aeon and it still would not be possible to finish, thus I have now explained it succinctly."

The Buddha said to Maitreya, "Those who are able to hear this Buddha's name, leap with joy, and recite this Buddha's name even once—know that—these beings will attain great benefit. Furthermore, this is endowed with unsurpassed meritorious virtue.

"For that reason, Maitreya, were there even a great conflagration that fully engulfed the three thousand great thousand realms, still you should cross it to hear this scriptural dharma, and with joy and ready faith, receive and keep, read and recite it, and practice in accord with its teachings. Why is this? There are many bodhisattvas who wish to hear this scripture, but are not able to do so. Should there be sentient beings who hear this scripture, they will not retrogress to the end of this unsurpassed path. For this reason you must dedicate your mind, believe, receive, keep, recite, and practice it as taught."

The Buddha said, "Now that I have expounded this scriptural dharma for all sentient beings, enabling them to see the Buddha of Infinite Life and that land with all within it, for that reason you should all strive to do what you should. You must not, after I have transcended from this world, again give rise to doubts. Although in future worlds, the path of my scripture will perish, due to my compassion and sympathy, this scripture in particular, I will leave in this world to remain for a hundred ages. Those sentient beings who encounter this scripture, and sincerely aspire, will all attain release."

The Buddha said to Maitreya, "It is difficult to encounter and difficult to see a tathāgata who has appeared in this world, and it is difficult to attain and difficult to hear the buddhas' path of the scripture. It is also difficult to be able to hear the excellent dharma of the bodhisattvas and of the pāramitās. To encounter a person of good knowledge, to hear the dharma and practice it, this too is difficult. But, if you should chance to hear this scripture, rejoice in it with faith, and receive and keep it, this is the most difficult amongst all difficulties; there being nothing more difficult than this.

"For that reason, according to my dharma, thus has the Buddha of Infinite Life done, thus as I have expounded, and thus as I have taught, therefore you must have faith and follow it, and practice in accord with this dharma."

At that time when the World Honored One expounded this scriptural dharma, immeasurable sentient beings all awakened the aspiration for supreme perfect enlightenment. Twelve thousands of vast numbers of mortals attained the pure dharma-eye; two billion and two hundred million celestials and humans attained the stage of non-returning; eight hundred thousand monks extinguished their defilements and liberated their minds to become arhats; and four billion bodhisattvas attained the stage of non-retrogression, adorned themselves with the merit of a great vow, and in a future world will attain perfect enlightenment.

At that time, three thousand great thousand worlds shook in six ways and a great light universally illuminated the lands of the ten directions, a hundred thousand sounds of music were spontaneously produced, and immeasurable exquisite flowers fluttered down in profusion. When the Buddha finished expounding this scripture, Maitreya Bodhisattva, along with the assembly of bodhisattvas from the ten directions, the elder Ānanda and the great śrāvakas, and the entirety of the great assembly, having heard this Buddha's expounding, all rejoiced without exception.

The Visualization of Infinite Life Sutra as Expounded by the Buddha

Translated into Chinese during the Liu-Song Dynasty
by Tripiṭaka Master Kālayaśas of Central Asia

Thus have I heard. At one time the Buddha was at Vulture Peak in the citadel of Rājagṛha, with a great assembly of monks numbering twelve hundred and fifty, and with bodhisattvas numbering thirty-two thousand led by Mañjuśrī, the Dharma Prince.

At one time there was a prince at Rājagṛha named Ajātaśatru. Informed by his evil friend, Devadatta, he seized his father, King Bimbisāra, and confined him to a room with seven-fold walls. Furthermore, he restrained the court ministers, so that not even one could approach the king.

The queen of the realm was named Vaidehī. She was devoted to the king, so she bathed and cleansed her body, spread it with gruel made of ghee and honey mixed with wheat, filled her jewelry with juice squeezed from grapes, and secretly presented it to the king. The king ate the gruel, drank the juice, then requested water to rinse his mouth. Having rinsed his mouth, he joined his palms in reverence, faced Vulture Peak, paying obeisance from afar to the World Honored One, and said, "Mahā-Maudgalyāyana is my close friend. I implore you to take pity on me and let him bestow upon me the eight precepts." At which, Maudgalyāyana flew swift as a hawk to the place of the king, and day after day administered the eight precepts. The World Honored One also sent the Venerable Pūrṇa to expound the dharma to the king. This continued for a period of three weeks of seven days with the king eating the gruel and listening to the dharma, whereby he appeared serene and content.

At that time, Ajātaśatru questioned the guard, "Is my father the king yet still alive?" Then guard replied, "Your Majesty, Queen Vaidehī spreads her body with gruel, fills her jewelry with juice, and provides this to the king. The śramaṇa ascetics Mahā-Maudgalyāyana and Pūrṇa come here through the air to expound the dharma to the king, and they cannot be barred from entry." When Ajātaśatru heard this account, he became furious with his mother, and said, "My mother is a conspirator, an accomplice to the other conspirators. The śramaṇa ascetics are evil people, who have used their magic powers to keep this evil king from dying these many days." Then suddenly Ajātaśatru took his sword in hand, intending to kill his mother.

At that time there was a minister, named Candraprabha, who was intelligent and wise. He, along with the Jīvaka, bowed to the king and addressed him saying, "Your Majesty, we ministers are well versed in the Veda scriptures, and from when aeons began until now though there have been eighteen thousand evil kings who have killed their fathers to usurp the throne, never have we heard of the atrocity of killing a mother. Your Majesty, if you now commit this outrageous act, you will sully the kṣatriya class, and we cannot bear to hear of this. This act would make you an outcaste and we could not allow you to remain as such." Then the two ministers, having said this, put their hands to their swords and stepped back.

At which, Ajātaśatru, terrified and panicked, addressed Jīvaka asking, "Are you not my ally?" Jīvaka replied, "Your Majesty, restrain yourself and do not kill your mother." When the king heard this, he repented begging for mercy. Then he immediately discarded his sword, and abandoned his attempt to kill his mother. He then ordered his palace ministers to lock his mother in an inner palace chamber so that she might never leave.

At this time when Vaidehī, thus confined, became haggard and despaired, she turned toward Vulture Peak, made obeisance to the Buddha from afar, and said, "Tathāgata, World Honored One, in the past you used to send Ānanda to come and console me. Now I am miserable and disconsolate, and though you yourself are so eminent it is unfeasible to see you, I wish that you might send Maudgalyāyana and the Venerable Ānanda to see me." When she finished saying this, she wept tears like pouring rain, and again made obeisance to the Buddha from afar. Even before she had finished raising her head, at that moment, the World Honored One on Vulture Peak knew the thoughts that Vaidehī held in her heart.

At once, the Buddha bade Maudgalyāyana and Ānanda to proceed through the air, and the Buddha vanished from Vulture Peak to reappear at the palace. As Vaidehī raised her head from paying obeisance, she saw the World Honored One, Śākyamuni Buddha. The Buddha's form was a purple-golden hue, and the Buddha sat on a lotus blossom of a hundred jewels. Maudgalyāyana attended the Buddha on the left and Ānanda on the right. Indra, Brahma, and the deva kings who protect the quarters of the world were in the air universally scattering celestial flowers like rain in offering to the Buddha.

When Vaidehī saw the Buddha, the World Honored One, she tore off her jewelry and threw herself to the ground. Sobbing, she turned to the Buddha and said, "World Honored One, what karmic burden of transgressions caused me to give birth to this evil son? World Honored One, what karmic cause and effect made Devadatta a relative of yours? I implore you, World Honored One, to tell me of a place of no sorrow and affliction where I may achieve birth. I do not want to be in this sordid and evil world of Jambudvīpa. This sordid and evil place is full of the realms of hell, hungry ghosts, and beasts, with many no-good rogues. I wish that I might never more hear evil words or see evil people. Now I face you, the World Honored One, and prostrate myself to the ground before you in repentance begging your mercy. I implore you, the Sun-like Buddha, to teach me to envision a place of pure conduct."

Then the World Honored One emitted a light from between his eyebrows. This light of gold color universally illuminated immeasurable worlds in the ten directions, then returned to rest upon the crown of the Buddha's head, where it transformed into a gold dais like Mount Sumeru. The pure and sublime lands of all the buddhas of the ten directions were manifested within it. There were lands formed of seven jewels and other lands entirely of lotuses. There were also lands like the palace of Maheśvara's heaven and lands like crystal mirrors. All of these lands of the ten directions were manifested within the dais. In this way, immeasurable buddha lands could be viewed in their splendor, and Vaidehī was able to see them.

Then Vaidehī said to the Buddha, "World Honored One, all of these buddha lands are alike in their pureness and all have radiant light, but now I would like to be born in the Land of Ultimate Beatitude, the place of Amitāyus Buddha. I implore you, World Honored One, to teach me its contemplation and teach me its correct attainment."

At which time, the World Honored One immediately smiled, emitting lights of five colors from his mouth. Each one of these lights then shined upon the crown of King Bimbisāra's head. Then the great King, who was locked up in confinement, found his mind's eye was freed of hindrances and he could see the World Honored One from afar. He bowed his head in reverence and spontaneously made spiritual progress to stage of non-returning.

Then the World Honored One said to Vaidehī, "Now, do you not know that Amitāyus Buddha is not far from here? You should dedicate your thoughts and envision this land. This is the pure conduct. Now I will explain for you in detail with illustrations. Furthermore, I will enable ordinary mortals in future worlds, who wish to practice the pure conduct, that they may attain birth in the Western Land of Ultimate Beatitude. Those who wish to be born in this land should practice the three acts of merit. The first is honoring one's father and mother, respecting one's teachers and elders, compassionately refraining from killing, and practicing the ten acts of virtuous conduct. The second is taking refuge in the Buddha, the Dharma, and the Saṃgha, keeping the precepts, and refraining from misconduct of the practices. The third is awakening to the aspiration for enlightenment, profoundly believing in the law of cause and effect, reading and reciting the Mahāyāna sutras, and encouraging others to endeavor on the path. These three acts are called the pure conduct." The Buddha said to Vaidehī, "Do you not know that these three forms of conduct are the true cause of pure conduct of all the buddhas of the three temporal realms of the past, present, and future?"

The Buddha said to both Ānanda and Vaidehī, "Listen carefully, listen carefully, and ponder this well. I, the Tathāgata, will now explain the pristine pure conduct for all sentient beings of future worlds, for they who are afflicted by the hindrances. Well done, Vaidehī, to have asked about this. Ānanda, you must receive and keep these words spoken by the Buddha, and disseminate them widely to the many sentient beings.

"I, the Tathāgata, will now teach Vaidehī and all sentient beings, even those of future worlds, how to envision the Western Land of Ultimate Beatitude. By the power of the Buddha, you should be able to see that pure and pristine land, like holding a clear mirror and seeing your own face reflected. Upon seeing that buddha land of ultimate sublimity and beatitude, you will rejoice at heart, and thereby at that instance immediately attain the insight of non-arising of phenomena."

The Buddha said to Vaidehī, "You are merely an ordinary mortal. Your heart and thoughts are distraught and confused, and you have yet to attain the divine eye, so cannot see afar. All the Buddhas, and I myself the Tathāgata, have special expedient devices by which to enable you to see."

Then, Vaidehī said to the Buddha, "World Honored One, in this way, by the power of the Buddha, I can now see that buddha land, but after the Buddha passes into ultimate transcendence, all the sentient beings—who suffer from the corruptions and evil acts, un-virtuous conduct, and the five sufferings how can they see Amitāyus Buddha, and the Land of Ultimate Beatitude?"

The Buddha said to Vaidehī, "You and the sentient beings should single-mindedly concentrate your thoughts and contemplate the west. How do you form this contemplation? In general, to form this contemplation, all sentient beings, unless born blind, have eyes with which they all can see the setting sun. You should commence this meditation by sitting in the proper position facing west and envision the sun. You should firmly establish it in your mind, focus on your contemplation without distraction, and view the sun as it is about to set in a form like a suspended drum. After you have completed viewing the sun, whether your eyes are open or closed, it should all be perfectly clear. This is the sun contemplation, called the First Visualization."

"Next form the water contemplation. View the water in its limpid purity, again until it is perfectly clear, and do not let your concentration be distracted. When you have finished viewing the water, then you should commence contemplating it frozen. View the ice in its translucence and contemplate it becoming the aquamarine jewel, beryl. When you have accomplished this contemplation, view the beryl ground as translucent from its surface to its depths. Below, there are adamantine bannered pillars of gold and the other seven jewels that support the beryl ground. These bannered pillars of the eight directions are endowed with eight facets, and each of these facets is formed of hundreds of jewels. Each one of these jewel pearls has a thousand rays of light, and each single ray of light shines with eighty-four thousand colors. These reflect off the beryl ground like a hundred billion suns, so that they cannot even be seen distinctly.

"Upon the beryl ground are gold cords laid out crossing to form sections, separate areas of the seven jewels, by which they are clearly distinguished. Each of these jewels has within it light of five hundred colors. The light is like florets, or the moon and stars. The light is suspended in the sky forming daises of radiant light for pavilions ten million in number, which are formed of a combination of a hundred jewels. On either side of these daises, each have ten billion floral banners and immeasurable musical instruments, forming an ethereal adornment. The eight pure breezes emanate from the radiant light, stirring the musical instruments to expound in music the teachings on suffering, emptiness, impermanence, and non-self. This is the water contemplation, called the Second Visualization."

"At the time you compose this contemplation, envision each individually until thoroughly clear, whether the eyes are opened or closed, and do not allow it be disordered. Except when sleeping, you should constantly recall it. The contemplation such as this is called the general view of the ground of the Land of Ultimate Beatitude. Should you achieve this samādhi and see the ground of this land in complete clarity, it would be indescribable. This is the ground contemplation, called the third visualization."

The Buddha said to Ānanda, "You should keep these Buddha words and expound this method of envisioning the ground for all the sentient beings of future worlds who wish to be released from their suffering. Those who envision this ground will extinguish the effect of the transgressions of eight billion aeons of reincarnations and when they shed their bodies in the mundane world, they will assuredly be born in the Pure Land. Harbor no doubts in your heart. The practice of this visualization is called the true visualization; should there be other visualizations, they would be called unorthodox visualizations."

The Buddha said to Ānanda and Vaidehī, "Having accomplished the ground contemplation, next envision the jewel trees. To envision the jewel trees, envision each individually, and form the contemplation of the seven layered rows of trees. Each individual tree is eight thousand yojanas in height. All these jewel trees have flowers and leaves of the seven jewels, without exception. Each individual flower and leaf forms diverging jewels and colors: the aquamarine beryl color emits from within a gold colored light; the rock-crystal color emits from within a crimson colored light; the cornelian color emits from within a white-shell light; the white-shell color emits from within a green pearl light, also coral and amber, all these jewels form decorous reflections.

"Exquisite pearl veils are hung over the trees, and each individual tree has seven layers of veils. Between each veil are fifty-billion exquisite floral palaces, akin to the palaces of the Brahma Heaven, with many celestial young acolytes naturally dwelling within. Each acolyte has fifty-billion cintāmaṇi jewels which form their jewelry. The light of the cintāmaṇi jewels illuminates for a hundred yojanas, verily like a combination of ten billion suns and moons, so as to be indescribable. All these jewels intermingling together form the most superior of colors.

"The jewel trees have each row appropriately spaced, with the leaves spaced accordingly. Between the leaves bloom exquisite flowers, and the flowers naturally give rise to fruits of seven jewels. Each leaf of the trees is twenty-five yojanas perfectly round in length and breadth. These leaves have a thousand colors and a hundred kinds of patterns, like celestial ornaments. This assembly of exquisite flowers forms the color of Jambū gold, as though encircled in a ring of fire between each leaf. The fruits they give birth to resemble Indra's vase. These have a great radiant light that transforms into banners and immeasurable jewel canopies. These jewel canopies reflect within all the Buddhist works of the three thousand, great thousand realms; the buddha worlds of the ten directions are likewise displayed within. Having seen the trees, you should envision this again one by one in order. Envision and see the trunks, branches, leaves, flowers, and fruits of the trees, until all is perfectly clear. This is the tree contemplation, called the fourth visualization."

"Next you should contemplate the water. In this contemplation of the water, the Land of Ultimate Beatitude has pools of water of eight virtues. Each one of these pools of water is made of the seven jewels, and these jewels are supple. They spring forth from the king of wish-fulfilling jewels, then fork into fourteen branches. Each of these branches forms colors of the seven jewels, with yellow gold forming the channels. The bottom of all the channels are all laid with diamonds of variegated colors forming the sand. Each of the waters has within it six billion lotus blossoms of seven jewels. Each of these lotus blossoms is perfectly round with a diameter of twelve yojanas.

"The cintāmaṇi water flows with fountains between the blossoms to flow up and down the trees. Its sound, in its exquisite delicacy, expounds the teachings on suffering, emptiness, impermanence, non-self, and the pāramitās, and moreover sings the praise of the major marks of the Buddha. The king of wish-fulfilling jewels emanates a gold colored radiant light of exquisite delicacy. This light transforms into birds of a hundred colors of jewels. Their beautiful harmonic voices constantly sing the praise of meditating on the Buddha, the Dharma, and the Saṃgha. This is the contemplation of the waters of eight virtues, called the fifth visualization."

"In this land of many jewels, every area has on it fifty billion jewel pavilions. Within these jewel pavilions there are immeasurable celestials making celestial music and dance. Moreover, there are musical instruments suspended in the air like celestial jewel banners, which do not need to be played, but produce their music spontaneously. This orchestra of sounds all expounds the meditation on the Buddha, the Dharma, and the Saṃgha. When this contemplation has been accomplished, it is called the overview of the Land of Ultimate Beatitude; the jewel trees, jewel ground, and jewel pools.

"This is the contemplation of the overall visualization, called the sixth visualization. Those who see this will eliminate innumerable aeons of extremely grave evil karma, and after their lives have ended, they will assuredly be born in this land. The practice of this visualization is called the true visualization; should there be other visualizations, they would be called unorthodox visualizations."

The Buddha said to Ānanda and Vaidehī, "Listen carefully, listen carefully, and ponder this well. I, the Buddha, shall expound to you in detail the way to eliminate suffering. You should keep and remember this, and transmit it to the great assembly of sentient beings by expounding it in detail."

At the moment the Buddha expounded this, the Buddha of Infinite Life appeared standing in midair with the two great lords Avalokiteśvara and Mahāsthāmaprāpta standing in accompaniment on the left and right. Their radiant light was so dazzling that the Buddha could not be seen distinctly. Even the hundred thousand times the colors of Jambū gold could not compare with it.

When Vaidehī saw the Buddha of Infinite Life, she paid homage at the Buddha's feet, and said to the Buddha, "World Honored One, I now due to the Buddha's power have attained sight of the Buddha of Infinite Life and the two bodhisattvas, but for the sentient beings of the future, how can they envision the Buddha of Infinite Life and the two bodhisattvas?"

The Buddha replied to Vaidehī, "Those who wish to envision this Buddha should commence this meditation. On the ground with seven jewels, form the contemplation of the lotus blossom. Have this lotus blossom, each individual petal, form jewels of a hundred colors. Each has eighty-four thousand lineaments, verily like a celestial painting, and each of these lineaments has eighty-four thousand lights. You should be able to see all, each in clear distinction.

"The smaller petals of the blossoms are two hundred and fifty yojanas in length and breadth, and as such, this lotus blossom has eighty-four thousand petals. In between each petal, each has ten billion of the king of cintāmaṇi jewels, which form decorous reflections. Each individual cintāmaṇi jewel emanates a thousand radiant lights. These lights are like canopies, made of a combination of the seven jewels, and which spread out universally over the land.

"A cintāmaṇi jewel forms the dais. This lotus blossom dais has eighty thousand diamonds, jewels red as the flowers of the kiṃśuka tree, Brahma jewels, and delicate pearl veils; all of which intermingle decorously. On this dais, naturally there are also four pillars of jewel banners. Each of these jewel banners is akin to a hundred thousand trillion Sumeru mountains. Above the banners are jewel streamers, verily akin to the palaces in the heaven of Yama, and each of these has fifty billion exquisitely delicate jewel pearls, which form decorous reflections. Each of these jewel pearls has eighty-four thousand lights, and each of these lights forms eighty-four thousand different kinds of gold colors. Each of these gold colors spreads out over the jewel ground making transformations here and there, changing into different forms, sometimes becoming diamond daises, or pearl veils, or various floral clouds. Throughout the ten directions, they change their appearance as willed to perform the work of the Buddha. This is the contemplation of the blossom seat, called the seventh visualization."

The Buddha said to Ānanda, "Such a marvelous blossom as this was made by the power of Dharmākara's original vow. Those who wish to meditate on this Buddha should first form the contemplation of this blossom seat. When forming this contemplation, you must not be careless in your visualization. All should be visualized one by one; each petal one by one, each pearl one by one, each light one by one, each dais one by one, each banner one by one. All these must be clearly distinct, like seeing your own image in a mirror. Those who accomplish this contemplation will extinguish the transgressions of fifty thousand aeons of reincarnations and will assuredly be born in the Land of Ultimate Beatitude. The practice of this visualization is called the true visualization; should there be other visualizations, they would be called unorthodox visualizations."

The Buddha said to Ānanda and Vaidehī, "Once you have seen this, next you should contemplate the Buddha. Why is that? All the Buddhas, the Tathāgatas, have bodies of the dharma realm, which enter into the mental contemplations arising in all sentient beings. For that reason, when you mentally contemplate the Buddha, your mind is exactly that, the thirty-two major marks and the eighty minor marks of the Buddha. Thus, the mind forms the Buddha; the mind is the Buddha. All the buddhas, who have the oceanic wisdom of universal truth, arise from this mental contemplation. Therefore, you should at once wholeheartedly dedicate your meditation to visualizing this Buddha, Tathāgata Arhat Samyak-saṃbuddha.

"To contemplate this Buddha, first contemplate the image. Whether your eyes are opened or closed, you should see a jewel image, the color of Jambū gold, seated on this blossom. Once you have seen this seated image, your mind's eye should attain awakening and you will see the Land of Ultimate Beatitude, completely and in clear distinction; the ethereal adornment of its seven jewels, the jewel ground, the jewel pond, the rows of jewel trees, the many celestial jewel streamers spread above them, and a profusion of jewel veils completely filling the sky. Seeing like this should be extremely clear, like visualizing your own palm.

"Once you have seen this, once again form another large lotus blossom to the left of the Buddha, just like the previous lotus blossom without any difference. Then form another large lotus blossom to the right of the Buddha. Contemplate a single image of Avalokiteśvara Bodhisattva seated on the left blossom seat, which emanates a gold light just as previous without any difference. Contemplate a single image of Mahāsthāmaprāpta Bodhisattva seated on the right blossom seat. When you accomplish this contemplation, the images of the Buddha and the Bodhisattvas all emanate radiant light. This light is the color of gold and illuminates the jewel trees. Under each individual tree, there are again three lotus blossoms. On these lotus blossoms, each has an image of a single Buddha and two Bodhisattvas, which completely fill the land throughout.

"When this contemplation is made, the practitioner should hear the flowing water, the radiant light, everything including the jewel trees and the birds and waterfowl, all of them expounding the sublime dharma. Whether out of samādhi or in samādhi, the sublime dharma is constantly heard. When the practitioner hears this even while not in samādhi, the memory will be retained and not be lost.

"This must be in accordance with the sutra. If it is not in accordance, it is called an illusory contemplation. If it is in accordance, it is called the provisional contemplation of seeing the Land of Ultimate Beatitude. This is the contemplation of the images, called the eighth visualization. Those who form this visualization will eliminate the transgressions of immeasurable aeons of reincarnations, and while still in their present body will attain the samādhi of meditating on the Buddha."

The Buddha said to Ānanda and Vaidehī, "Having accomplished this contemplation, next you should then envision the Buddha of Infinite Life's bodily marks and radiant light. Ānanda, you should know that the body of the Buddha of Infinite Life is a color like a hundred quadrillion Jambū grains of gold in Yama's heaven. The height of the Buddha's body is in yojanas of some sixty-trillion vast number multiplied by the number of sands of the Ganges River. The white swirl of hair between the Buddha's eyebrows curls to the right and is akin to five Sumeru mountains. The Buddha's eyes are like the waters of the four great seas, with the blue and white clearly differentiated. The hair follicles of the Buddha's body emanate radiant light akin to Mount Sumeru. This Buddha's round nimbus is like ten billion of the three thousand, great thousand realms, and within this round nimbus are transformed buddhas of some hundred trillion vast numbers multiplied by the number of the sands of the Ganges River. Each of these transformed buddhas again has an assembly of vast innumerable transformed bodhisattvas who accompany them.

"The Buddha of Infinite Life has eighty-four thousand major marks and each one of these marks has eighty-four thousand minor marks. Each of these minor marks moreover has eighty-four thousand radiant lights. Each of these radiant lights universally illuminates the realms in the ten directions, embracing all and forsaking none of the sentient beings reciting the Buddha's name. The radiant light, the major and minor marks, extending even to the transformed buddhas, are all indescribable.

"You should, moreover, elicit this contemplation and see it in the mind's eye. Seeing this is equivalent to seeing all the buddhas of the ten directions. Due to seeing all the buddhas, this is called the samādhi of meditating on the buddha. Forming this visualization is called the visualization of the bodies of all the buddhas. By envisioning the buddha body, you also see the buddha mind. The buddha mind is great compassion itself, of limitless mercy in the salvation of all sentient beings. Those who practice this visualization, when they discard their bodies for the other world, they will be reborn before the Buddha and attain the insight of non-arising of phenomena.

"For that reason, a Wise One should dedicate their mind to perceiving the Buddha of Infinite Life. To envision the Buddha of Infinite Life is to enter by one of the minor and major marks of the Buddha. Simply envision the white swirl of hair between the Buddha's eyebrows until it is extremely clear. Should the white swirl of hair between the eyebrows be seen, then the eighty-four thousand major and minor marks of the Buddha will naturally appear. To see the Buddha of Infinite Life is to see all the immeasurable buddhas of the ten directions. Having attained this sight of all the immeasurable buddhas, all the buddhas manifested before one will bestow the prediction of future enlightenment. This is the contemplation of visualizing all the physical features of the Buddha's body, called the ninth visualization. The practice of this visualization is called the true visualization; should there be any other visualizations, they would be called unorthodox visualizations."

The Buddha said to Ānanda and Vaidehī, "Once you have seen the Buddha of Infinite Life Buddha completely and in clear distinction, next you should then envision Avalokiteśvara Bodhisattva. This Bodhisattva's body is some eighty trillion vast number of yojanas in height. The Bodhisattva has a body the color of purple-gold, an uṣṇīṣa cranial protuberance on the crown of the head, and a round nimbus at the nape, which is a hundred thousand yojanas in each direction. Within this nimbus are five hundred transformed buddhas resembling Śākyamuni Buddha. Each of these transformed buddhas again has five hundred transformed bodhisattvas, who are accompanied by immeasurable celestial deities. The light emanating from the Bodhisattva's body has within it the sentient beings of the five paths, all of whom are manifested in the entirety of their aspects.

"On the top of this Bodhisattva's head is a cintāmaṇi jewel, which forms the Bodhisattva's celestial crown. Within this celestial crown, there is a standing transformed buddha with the height of twenty-five yojanas. The face of Avalokiteśvara is the color of Jambū gold. The swirl of hair between the Bodhisattva's eyebrows is endowed with the colors of the seven jewels, and from which flows forth eighty-four thousand kinds of radiant lights. Each individual radiant light has immeasurable, innumerable hundreds of thousands of transformed buddhas, and each one of these transformed buddhas has innumerable transformed bodhisattvas who accompany them. They change their manifestations freely to fill the worlds of the ten directions. They are like the hue of the red lotus blossom.

"The Bodhisattva has eight billion radiant lights forming the Bodhisattva's ornaments. These ornaments universally manifest the entirety of the ethereal adornment of that land. The palms of Avalokiteśvara's hands form fifty billion assorted colors of lotus blossoms. The hands have ten fingertips and each one of these fingertips has eighty-four thousand patterns verily like a printed design. Each one of these patterns has eighty-four thousand colors, and each one of these colors has eighty-four thousand lights. These lights are supple and illuminate everywhere universally, whereby Avalokiteśvara's jewel hands rescue the sentient beings.

"Upon lifting the foot, the bottom of Avalokiteśvara's foot has the mark of a thousand-spoke cakra wheel, which naturally transforms into fifty billion daises of radiant light. Upon setting the foot down, adamantine and cintāmaṇi flowers scatter everywhere leaving nothing uncovered. Avalokiteśvara is endowed with all the rest of the major and minor bodily marks just like the Buddha with no difference. Only Avalokiteśvara's uṣṇīṣa and the invisible cranial mark is not up to the World Honored One's. This is the visualization of Avalokiteśvara Bodhisattva, the contemplation of the true physical features of Avalokiteśvara's body, called the tenth visualization."

The Buddha said to Ānanda, "Those who wish to envision Avalokiteśvara Bodhisattva should practice this visualization. Those who practice this visualization will not encounter misfortune, they will be cleansed of karmic hindrances, and the effect of their transgressions of innumerable aeons of reincarnations will be eliminated. Just hearing the name of a bodhisattva such as this one will reap immeasurable merit; how much more so if you perceive the Bodhisattva.

"Those who wish to envision Avalokiteśvara should first visualize the uṣṇīṣa cranial protuberance, and then visualize the celestial crown. The rest of the bodily marks should be visualized in order until completely clear as visualizing your own palm. The practice of this visualization is called the true visualization; should there be any other visualizations, they would be called unorthodox visualizations."

"Next you should then envision Mahāsthāmaprāpta Bodhisattva. The size of this Bodhisattva's body is the same as Avalokiteśvara. The Bodhisattva's round nimbus is a hundred and twenty-five yojanas in each direction, and illuminates for two hundred and fifty yojanas. The radiant light from the Bodhisattva's body illuminates the lands of the ten directions forming a purple-gold color, and those sentient beings with a karmic bond are all able to see it. Just seeing this Bodhisattva, the light from each hair follicle, is the same as seeing the pure and sublime radiant lights of all the immeasurable buddhas of the ten directions. For that reason this Bodhisattva is called Boundless Light. This light of wisdom illuminates all sentient beings universally to separate them from the three realms of defilement; thus are the superior powers attained by Mahāsthāmaprāpta. For that reason this Bodhisattva is called Great Force.

"This Bodhisattva's celestial crown has five hundred jewel blossoms, and each individual blossom has five hundred jewel daises. Within each one of these daises is manifested the appearance, in all their broad expanse, of the pure and sublime lands of the all buddhas of the ten directions. The uṣṇīṣa on the top of this Bodhisattva's head is like a red lotus blossom, and on it there is a jewel vase which brims with radiant light that universally manifests all the Buddhist works. The remainder of this Bodhisattva's bodily marks are just like Avalokiteśvara's with no difference.

"When this Bodhisattva moves, all the realms of the ten directions quake in entirety, and where the earth quakes, each has five hundred million of jewel blossoms. Each one of these jewel blossoms exhibits the height of ethereal adornment, like the Land of Ultimate Beatitude. When this Bodhisattva sits, the lands of seven jewels all quake at once, from the land of the Buddha of Golden Light below to the land of the Buddha of Royal Radiant Light above. From within these buddha lands, in immeasurable numbers like motes of dust, transformed bodies of the Buddha of Infinite Life, Avalokiteśvara, and Mahāsthāmaprāpta all gather together like clouds in the sky above the Land of Ultimate Beatitude. There they sit on lotus daises and expound the sublime dharma for the suffering sentient beings.

"The practice of this visualization is called the true visualization; should there be any other visualizations, they would be called unorthodox visualizations. To see Mahāsthāmaprāpta Bodhisattva, this is to visualize the contemplation of the hue and form of Mahāsthāmaprāpta, called the eleventh visualization. Visualizing this Bodhisattva eliminates the effect of transgressions of innumerable aeons of countless reincarnations. Those who practice this visualization will not be born in a womb, but already enjoy traverse the pure and sublime lands of all the buddhas. Having accomplished this visualization, it is called the endowments of Avalokiteśvara and Mahāsthāmaprāpta."

"When you have seen this, you should conceive yourself being born in the Western Land of Ultimate Beatitude, inside a lotus blossom seated in a cross-legged position. Form the contemplation of the closing of the lotus blossom, and then form the contemplation of the opening of the lotus blossom. When the lotus blossom opens, there will be lights of five hundred colors that enter to illuminate your body. Contemplate your eyes opening, then contemplate seeing the buddhas and bodhisattvas filling the sky. From the water, birds, trees, and groves to the buddhas, all intone the sublime dharma of all the twelve categories of sutras. Even when not in samādhi, the memory of this should be retained and not lost. Having seen this, it is called seeing the Buddha of Infinite Life and the Land of Ultimate Beatitude. This becomes the contemplation of universal contemplation, called the twelfth visualization. The Buddha of Infinite Life transformed into innumerable bodies, accompanied by Avalokiteśvara and Mahāsthāmaprāpta, will always come to the place where the person is practicing."

The Buddha said to Ānanda and Vaidehī, "Those who sincerely wish to be born in the Western Land should first visualize a sixteen-foot image on a pool of water. As explained previously, the Buddha of Infinite Life has a body of immeasurable dimensions, beyond the mental powers of ordinary mortals. However, through powers of this Tathāgata's original vow, those who elicit this contemplation will assuredly be able to achieve it. Just by contemplating the Buddha's image, one attains immeasurable merit; how much more so if you visualize the bodily marks by which the Buddha is endowed. Amitāyus Buddha has the supernormal powers to manifest anything as willed, whereby this Buddha can manifest as any form freely throughout the lands of the ten directions; at times manifesting a giant body that completely fills the sky, or manifesting a small body sixteen or eight feet in size. However the Buddha's form is manifested, it is always a gold color. From the transformed buddhas in the nimbus to the jewel lotus blossom, all are as explained above. Avalokiteśvara Bodhisattva and Mahāsthāmaprāpta are everywhere likewise the same in body. Sentient beings just by visualizing the marks of the head portion would know that this is Avalokiteśvara, or know that this is Mahāsthāmaprāpta. These two Bodhisattvas assist Amitāyus Buddha and universally edify all sentient beings. This is the manifold contemplation, called the thirteenth visualization."

The Buddha said to Ānanda and Vaidehī, "Those of the highest birth in the highest level are those sentient beings who make a vow to be born in that land, and give rise to the three kinds of mind which is a surety for achieving birth. What are these three? The first one is the sincere mind, the second is the profound mind, and the third is the mind of transferring merit in aspiration for birth in the Pure Land. Those endowed with these three minds will assuredly be born in that land.

"Moreover, there are three kinds of sentient beings who will achieve birth. What are these three? The first is those with a mind of compassion who do not kill, and are endowed with the practices of the precepts. The second is those who read and recite the sutras and commentaries of Mahāyāna Buddhism. The third is those who practice the six kinds of mindfulness. These vow to transfer their merit, aspire to birth in that land, and being endowed with this virtue will within one to seven days assuredly achieve birth.

"When they are born in that land, due to their overwhelming religious endeavors, Amitāyus Tathāgata will be accompanied by Avalokiteśvara and Mahāsthāmaprāpta, innumerable transformed buddhas, hundreds of thousands of monks—a great assembly of śrāvakas, innumerable celestials, and seven-jewel palaces. Avalokiteśvara holding an adamantine dais, and accompanied by Mahāsthāmaprāpta, will come before the practitioner. Amitāyus Buddha will emanate a great radiant light illuminating the practitioner's body and, accompanied by the bodhisattvas, will extend hands to greet the practitioner. Avalokiteśvara and Mahāsthāmaprāpta accompanied by innumerable bodhisattvas will sing the praises of and rouse the heart of the practitioner. Once the practitioner has seen this, the practitioner will leap with joy and will see their own body mount the adamantine dais. Following after the Buddha, in a snap of the fingers, the practitioner will achieve birth in that land.

"Once born in that land, the practitioner will see the hue of the Buddha's body, in all its marks with which it is endowed. The practitioner will see the hue and marks with which all the bodhisattvas are endowed. The radiant light, the jewel trees expound the sublime dharma in song. Hearing this, the practitioner immediately awakens to the insight of the non-arising of phenomena. In the space of a moment, the practitioner makes offerings to all the buddhas of the worlds in the ten directions. Before all the buddhas, the practitioner then receives the prediction of future enlightenment. Then back in the Land of Ultimate Beatitude, the practitioner attains the gate to dhāraṇīs, in immeasurable hundreds of thousands. This is called the highest birth of the highest level."

"Those of the middle birth of the highest level are those who may not have completely managed to receive, keep, read, and recite all of the Mahāyāna sutras, but have well understood their essence, their hearts are not disturbed by the first principle of reality, they profoundly believe in cause and effect, and do not revile the teachings of the Mahāyāna. This merit they then vow to transfer in aspiration for birth in the Land of Ultimate Beatitude.

"Those who practice this conduct, when their lives come to an end, Amitāyus Buddha accompanied by Avalokiteśvara and Mahāsthāmaprāpta, surrounded by an immeasurable great entourage, will extend a purple-gold dais before the practitioner and proclaim in song, 'You, disciple of the dharma, have practiced the teachings of the Mahāyāna and understood the first principle. For that reason, we have now come to greet you.' Then a thousand transformed buddhas all at once extend their hands, and the practitioner sees oneself seated on the purple-gold dais. The practitioner clasps their palms together with fingers interwoven and singing the praise of all the buddhas, in a moment of thought is immediately born in that land in the pond of seven jewels.

"The purple-gold dais is like a great jewel lotus and overnight already opens. The practitioner's body becomes the color of polished purple-gold with a seven-jewel lotus immediately underfoot. The Buddha and Bodhisattvas all at once emanate a radiant light illuminating the body of the practitioner, whose eyes then immediately open. Due to the cause of the practices of the former lifetime, the practitioner hears the host of voices universally expounding the profound first principle. The practitioner then descends from the gold dais to pay respect to the Buddha with palms clasped and sings the praise of the World Honored One. After seven days have passed, the practitioner already attains the stage of non-retrogression for supreme perfect enlightenment. At that time, the practitioner attains the talent to fly throughout the ten directions and pay visits to all the buddhas, where at the site of the buddha, the practitioner practices the many samādhi and over the course of one minor aeon attains the insight of non-arising of phenomena and the prediction of becoming a buddha. This is called the middle birth of the highest level."

"Those of the lowest birth of the highest level are those who once again believe in cause and effect and do not revile the teachings of the Mahāyāna, but have merely awakened to the aspiration for the unsurpassed path. This merit they then vow to transfer in aspiration for birth in the Land of Ultimate Beatitude.

"These practitioners, when their lives come to an end, Amitāyus Buddha along with Avalokiteśvara, Mahāsthāmaprāpta, and accompanied by the entourage will extend a gold lotus blossom. Along with five hundred transformation buddhas that are manifested, they come to greet this person. These five hundred buddhas will all at once reach out their hands and proclaim in song, 'You, disciple of the dharma, are now purified and have awakened to the aspiration for the unsurpassed path. Hence, we have come to greet you.' Upon seeing this, the practitioner sees oneself already seated on a gold lotus blossom.

"Once seated, the lotus blossom closes, and the practitioner follows after the World Honored One to immediately achieve birth in the seven-jewel pond. After a day and a night, the lotus blossom then opens, and within seven days the practitioner then attains sight of the Buddha. However, the Buddha's form is not clearly discerned, and the marks of the Buddha are not clear in the mind, but after three weeks of seven days have passed, they are seen clearly. The practitioner hears a host of voices all singing the sublime dharma. The practitioner traverses in the ten directions to pay homage to all the buddhas and before all the buddhas is able to hear the profound dharma. After three minor aeons have passed, the practitioner attains the gate to a hundred dharmas and dwells in the ground of exuberant joy. This is called the lowest birth of the highest level. This is called the contemplation of the birth of the superior aspirants, called the fourteenth visualization."

The Buddha said to Ānanda and Vaidehī, "Those of the highest birth in the middle level are those sentient beings who have received and kept the five precepts, kept the eight precepts, and also practice the many other precepts, have not committed the five grave offenses, nor other transgressions. These roots of goodness, they then vow to transfer in aspiration for birth in the Western Land of Ultimate Beatitude.

"When their lives come to an end, Amitāyus Buddha accompanied by the monks and surrounded by an entourage will emit a gold colored light and reach the person's place to expound the dharmas of suffering, emptiness, impermanence, and non-self, and sing in praise renunciation of lay life whereby attaining leave of a host of suffering. Having seen this, the practitioner's heart is filled with great exuberant joy. The practitioner then sees oneself seated on the lotus-blossom dais. The practitioner makes a long bow with palms clasped together in reverence to the Buddha. Before the practitioner raises one's head, the practitioner immediately achieves birth in the Land of Ultimate Beatitude, and the lotus blossom promptly opens. When the blossom opens, the practitioner hears a host of voices singing praise of the four noble truths. At that time, the practitioner immediately attains the path of the arhat, thus acquiring the six spiritual powers and the three kinds of clairvoyance, and the eight kinds of emancipation. This is called the highest birth of the middle level."

"Those of the middle birth in the middle level are those sentient beings who have received and kept the eight precepts for a day and a night, or kept the precepts of a novice for a day and a night, or kept the full precepts of an ordinand for a day and a night, and do not neglect to maintain proper deportment. This merit they then vow to transfer in aspiration for birth in the Land of Ultimate Beatitude.

"Those practitioners such as this, whose practices of the precepts permeate them like incense, when their lives come to an end, they will see Amitāyus Buddha, accompanied by an entourage emitting a gold colored light and carrying a seven-jewel lotus blossom to extend before the practitioner. The practitioner will hear voices in the sky proclaim in song, 'For a good person such as yourself, you Good Son, who have followed the teachings of all the buddhas of the three periods, thus have we come to greet you.' The practitioner sees oneself seated on the lotus blossom, which immediately closes, and is born in the Western Land of Ultimate Beatitude in the jewel pond. Then after a period of seven days, the lotus blossom opens. Once the lotus blossom opens, the practitioner opens their eyes, clasps their palms together, and sings the praise of the World Honored One. The practitioner is overjoyed to hear the dharma and attains the first stage of the śrāvaka path, and after half an aeon has passed, the practitioner becomes an arhat. This is called the middle birth of the middle level."

"Those of the lowest birth in the middle level are those good sons and good daughters who pay filial respect to their fathers and mothers, and practice the benevolence and mercy of the mundane world. For these persons, when their lives are nearing their end, they have the chance to encounter a person of good knowledge, who for them expounds on the beatitude of Amitāyus Buddha's land, and also expounds the forty-eight vows of Dharmākara. Having heard this, their life promptly comes to an end, and in the space of the time it takes for a robust youth to curl and extend his arm, already are they born in the Western Land of Ultimate Beatitude. After seven days have passed since they were born, they encounter Avalokiteśvara and Mahāsthāmaprāpta, and hear the dharma with exuberant joy. After one minor aeon has passed, they become an arhat. This is called the lowest birth of the middle level. This is called the contemplation of the birth of the intermediate aspirants, called the fifteenth visualization."

The Buddha said to Ānanda and Vaidehī, "Those of the highest birth in the lowest level are those sentient beings who have formed a host of evil karma. Though they do not malign the myriad sutras, still deluded people such as these frequently carry out a host of evils without repentance. When their lives are nearing their end, they chance to encounter a person of good knowledge, who for them chants the titles of the twelve categories of the Mahāyāna sutras. Having heard in this way the names of the sutras, they eliminate a thousand aeons of extremely grave evil karma. This wise person then teaches them to clasp their palms together with fingers interwoven and intone 'Namo 'midabuddha.' By intoning the Buddha's name, they eliminate the effect of transgressions of five billion aeons of reincarnations.

"At that time, that Buddha will immediately send the Buddha's transformed buddha with the transformed Avalokiteśvara and transformed Mahāsthāmaprāpta to come before the practitioner and proclaim in song, 'Good Son, because you have intoned the Buddha's name, you have extinguished the effect of your many transgressions and we have come to greet you.' Once this has been spoken, the practitioner immediately sees the transformed buddha's radiant light extending to fill the room. Having seen this, the practitioner is exuberantly joyous and their life promptly comes to an end.

"They are carried on a jewel lotus blossom and follow immediately behind the transformed buddha to be born in the jewel pond. After seven weeks of seven days have passed, the lotus blossom opens. At the time the blossom opens, the great merciful Avalokiteśvara Bodhisattva and Mahāsthāmaprāpta emanate a great radiant light to settle before this person to expound for them the profound twelve categories of sutras. Having heard this, they have faith and understanding, and awaken to the aspiration for the unsurpassed path. After ten minor aeons have passed, they are bequeathed with the gate of a hundred dharmas, and attain entrance to the first stage of the bodhisattva path.

"This is called the highest birth of the lowest level. To be able to hear the name of the buddha, the name of the dharma, and the name of the saṃgha, hearing the name of the three treasures, is immediately to achieve birth."

The Buddha said to Ānanda and Vaidehī, "Those of the middle birth in the lowest level are those sentient beings who have violated the five precepts, the eight precepts, and the full precepts of an ordinand. Deluded people such as these have stolen possessions of the saṃgha, stolen donations to the saṃgha, have sullied the dharma by expounding it for personal gain, and have no repentance. Thus, does their evil karma display itself. These evil people, due to their evil acts, will as a result fall into hell.

"When their lives come to an end, they will meet the fires of hell until a time when they encounter a person of good knowledge. This person will out of great mercy for them expound on the virtue of the ten powers of Amitāyus Buddha, expound broadly on the divine power of that Buddha's radiant light, and sing in praise on the precepts, samādhi, wisdom, emancipation, and the knowledge and sight of the emancipation nirvana. When this person has heard this, the effect of transgressions of eight billion aeons of reincarnations will be eliminated. The roaring fires of hell will transform becoming pure cooling winds blowing celestial blossoms. All these blossoms have on them transformed buddhas and transformed bodhisattvas who come to greet this person. In an instant of thought, this person immediately achieves birth, and thus remains within a lotus blossom in the seven-jewel pond, until after six aeons have passed, and the lotus blossom opens. Just when the lotus blossom opens, Avalokiteśvara and Mahāsthāmaprāpta with pure clear voices will comfort this person, and for them expound the profound sutras of the Mahāyāna. Having heard the dharma, at once the person already awakens the aspiration for the unsurpassed path. This is called the middle birth of the lowest level."

The Buddha said to Ānanda and Vaidehī, "Those of the lowest birth of the lowest level are those sentient beings who have formed the non-virtuous conduct of committing the five grave offenses and the ten evil acts, along with various other non- virtuous acts. Such deluded people as these, due to their evil karma, will as a result fall into the unfortunate paths and pass a great number of aeons there, where they will incur suffering without end. "Such deluded people as these, when their lives come to an end, they will encounter a person of good knowledge, who will comfort them in many ways, explaining the sublime dharma for their sake and teaching them to meditate on the Buddha. Should these people be oppressed by suffering and unable to tranquilly meditate on the Buddha, that good friend would tell them, 'If you are unable to meditate, then rely on intoning the Buddha of Infinite Life.' In this way, they dedicate their minds and are able to voice without cessation the ten recitations of 'Namo 'midabuddha.' Due to intoning this Buddha's name, as they recite one by one, they eliminate the effect of transgressions of eight billion aeons of reincarnations.

"When their life comes to an end, they will see a gold lotus blossom verily like the orb of the sun residing right before the person. In an instant of thought, they immediately achieve birth in the Land of Ultimate Beatitude within a lotus blossom that will open after twelve major aeons have been fulfilled. Avalokiteśvara and Mahāsthāmaprāpta, with great merciful voices, will broadly expound for them the true aspect of all phenomena and the way to extinguish transgressions. Having heard this, they are overcome with joy, at which time they immediately awaken to the aspiration for enlightenment. This is called the lowest birth of the lowest level. This is called the contemplation of the birth of the inferior aspirants, called the sixteenth visualization."

At the time these words were expounded, Vaidehī along with her five hundred women attendants, as they heard the Buddha expound this, already at that time they saw the Land of Ultimate Beatitude, the breadth and length in all its aspects. They attained sight of the Buddha's form and that of the two Bodhisattvas. Their hearts gave rise to exuberant joy and they applauded as never before. They experienced the sudden awakening of great enlightenment and attained the insight of non-arising of phenomena. The five hundred women attendants awakened to the aspiration for supreme perfect enlightenment and aspired to be born in that land. The World Honored One bestowed on them the prediction that they would all assuredly achieve birth, and having been born in that land, attain samādhi in front of all the buddhas. The immeasurable numbers of celestials awakened to the aspiration for the unsurpassed path.

At that time, Ānanda rose from his seat and before the Buddha said, "World Honored One, what is the name of this sutra? How should the essence of this dharma be received and kept?"

The Buddha said to Ānanda, "This sutra's name is 'The Visualization of the Land of Ultimate Beatitude, The Buddha of Infinite Life, Avalokiteśvara Bodhisattva, and Mahāsthāmaprāpta Bodhisattva.' It is also called 'The Cleansing of the Hindrances of Karma and The Arising before All the Buddhas.' You should keep and receive this, and never forget it. Those who practice this samādhi will with their present body attain sight of the Buddhas of Infinite Life and the two Great Bodhisattvas. Should there be good sons and good daughters who merely hear this Buddha's name and the names of the two Bodhisattvas, they will eliminate the effect of transgressions of immeasurable aeons of reincarnations. How much more so if they maintain constant mindfulness! Should there be those who intone the Buddha's name, you should know that these people are like the puṇḍarīka among people. Avalokiteśvara and Mahāsthāmaprāpta will be their superior friends. They shall sit in the seat of enlightenment, and be born in the abode of the buddhas."

The Buddha said to Ānanda, "You should keep well these words. To keep these words is to keep the name of the Buddha of Infinite Life." When the Buddha expounded these words, from the venerables Maudgalyāyana and Ānanda extending to Vaidehī and the rest, upon hearing this expounding by the Buddha, all were greatly exuberantly overjoyed.

At that time, the Buddha, walking on air, returned to Vulture Peak. At which time, Ānanda then recounted for the great assembly all that had transpired. From the immeasurable number of celestials to the dragon beings and the yakṣas, upon hearing what was expounded by the Buddha, all were greatly exuberantly overjoyed, and paid homage to the Buddha from afar.

The Amitāyus Sutra
as Expounded by the Buddha

Translated into Chinese during the Yao-Qin Dynasty
by Tripiṭaka Master Kumārajīva of Kucha

Thus have I heard. At one time the Buddha was at the Jetavana garden in Śrāvastī, accompanied by a great assembly of monks, twelve hundred and fifty members in number. All these were well-known great arhats. Among them, the elders Śāriputra, Mahāmaudgalyāyana, Mahākāśyapa, Mahākātyāyana, Mahākauṣṭhila, Revata, Śuddhipanthaka, Nanda, Ānanda, Rāhula, Gavāṃpati, Piṇḍola Bharadvāja, Kālodayin, Mahākapphiṇa, Vakkula, and Aniruddha, were outstanding disciples. There was also a vast number of bodhisattvas, mahāsattvas; the most excellent among them were the Dharma Prince Mañjuśrī, the Bodhisattva Ajita, the Bodhisattva Gandhahastin, and the Bodhisattva Nityodyukta. In addition, innumerable celestials such as Indra had gathered.

At that time the Buddha said to the elder Śāriputra, "In the far west, as many as ten trillion buddha-lands away, there is a world called Ultimate Beatitude and in that land there is a buddha whose name is Amitāyus, who is even now there expounding the dharma. Śāriputra, do you know why that land is called Ultimate Beatitude? The sentient beings there have no suffering and experience only bliss. For that reason it is called Ultimate Beatitude.

"Also, Śāriputra, the Land of Ultimate Beatitude has seven tiers of balustrades, with seven layers of delicate veils, on trees of seven levels. All are set with four kinds of jewels, which adorn the world throughout. For that reason, this land is called Ultimate Beatitude.

"Again, Śāriputra, the Land of Ultimate Beatitude has pools of seven jewels, filled to the brim with water of eight virtues. The bottom of these pools are lined with sands of gold. The pools are surrounded by steps on their four sides made of gold, silver, aquamarine beryl, and crystal. Above are pavilions resplendently adorned with gold, silver, aquamarine beryl, rock-crystal, coral, red pearls, and cornelian. Within the pools are lotus blossoms as large as the wheels of a carriage. Those of blue color emit a blue light, those of yellow color emit a yellow light, those of red color emit a red light, and those of white color emit a white light. They are exquisitely sublime with a pristine fragrance. Śāriputra, the Land of Ultimate Beatitude is established such as this in virtue and ethereal adornment.

"Moreover, Śāriputra, in that Buddha's land, there is a constant playing of celestial music, and the land is made of yellow gold. Six times day and night, mandarava blossoms rain down. Every morning in the early quiet, the sentient beings of that land gather the exquisite blossoms into their flower baskets to make offerings to ten trillion buddhas in the other directions. When it is time for their meal, they instantly return home for their repast and a restful stroll. Śāriputra, the Land of Ultimate Beatitude is established such as this in virtue and ethereal adornment.

"Furthermore, Śāriputra, in the land of Ultimate Beatitude there is a constant variety of exotic birds of brilliant coloring, such as white egrets, peacocks, parrots, śārikās, kalaviṅkas, and jīvaṃjīvakas. The birds sing six times day and night with sounds of harmonious elegance. Their voices expound the Five Roots of Goodness, the Five Powers, the Seven Factors of Enlightenment, and the Noble Eightfold Path. The sentient beings of that land, upon hearing these voices, all become mindful of the Buddha, the Dharma, and the Saṃgha.

"Śāriputra, do not assume that these were born as birds as a result of transgressions in former lives. Why is this? This Buddha's land does not have the three unfortunate destinies. Śāriputra, in this Buddha's land, there are not even names for these three unfortunate destinies, how then could they exist? Amitāyus Buddha manifested all these birds through transformation so that they would transmit the sounds of the dharma through their songs.

"Śāriputra, in that Buddha's land, a subtle breeze wafts stirring the rows of jewel trees and their jewel veils, emitting a delicately sublime sound. This is just as though hundreds of thousands of musical instruments were being played in unison. Those who hear this melody all naturally devote their minds to being mindful of the Buddha, the Dharma, and the Saṃgha. Śāriputra, the Land of Ultimate Beatitude is established such as this in virtue and ethereal adornment.

"Śāriputra, why do you suppose this Buddha is called Amitāyus? Śāriputra, this Buddha' radiant light is immeasurable and it illuminates the worlds of the ten directions without hindrance. For that reason, this Buddha is called Amitāyus. In addition, Śāriputra, the lifespan of this Buddha and the denizens of that land are of immeasurable, boundless, incalculable aeons. For that reason, this Buddha is called Amitāyus. Śāriputra, from when Amitāyus Buddha achieved enlightenment until the present, ten aeons have already passed.

"Moreover, Śāriputra, this Buddha has an immeasurable boundless number of śrāvaka disciples. They are all arhats in numbers so vast as to be unknowable by calculation. Likewise so are the bodhisattvas. Śāriputra, the Land of Ultimate Beatitude is established such as this in virtue and ethereal adornment.

"Furthermore, Śāriputra, those sentient beings born in the Land of Ultimate Beatitude will all reach the stage of non-retrogression, and the vast majority the stage of attaining buddhahood in their next life. Their numbers are so vast as to be unknowable by calculation, and can only be explained in terms of immeasurable, boundless, incalculable aeons.

"Śāriputra, those sentient beings who hear this should awaken to the aspiration to be born in that land. Why is this? Should they attain this, they would be in the same place and encounter many superior good people. Birth cannot be achieved in that land with only minor roots of good and the merit of cause and effect.

"Śāriputra, should good men and good women hear of the teaching of Amitāyus Buddha and assiduously recite the Buddha's name for one day, two days, three, four, five, six, or seven days, single-heartedly without distraction, then when their lives come to an end, Amitāyus Buddha accompanied by an entourage of sages will appear before them. When their life ends, their minds will not be distracted, and they will immediately achieve birth in Amitāyus Buddha's Land of Ultimate Beatitude. Śāriputra, because I see the efficacy of this, that is why I say that should there be sentient beings who hear this teaching, they should aspire to be born in this land.

"Śāriputra, as I have now praised the ineffable virtue of Amitāyus Buddha, so are there buddhas to the east such as Akṣobhya Buddha, Merudhvaja Buddha, Mahāmeru Buddha, Meruprabhāsa Buddha, and Mañjudhvaja Buddha as numerous as the sands of the Ganges River. Each from their own lands has extended their vast tongues encompassing three thousand, great thousand realms, pronouncing these words of truth: 'Sentient beings, you should all believe in this discourse, The Praise of the Ineffable Virtue and Protection by All Buddhas.'

"Śāriputra, there are buddhas to the south such as Candra Sūryapradīpa Buddha, Yaśasprabha Buddha, Mahārciskandha Buddha, Merupradīpa Buddha, and Anantavīrya Buddha as numerous as the sands of the Ganges River. Each from their own lands, has extended their vast tongues encompassing three thousand, great thousand realms, pronouncing these words of truth: 'Sentient beings, you should all believe in this discourse, The Praise of the Ineffable Virtue and Protection by All Buddhas.'

"Śāriputra, there are buddhas to the west such as Amitāyus Buddha, Amitaketu Buddha, Amitadhvaja Buddha, Mahāprabha Buddha, Mahāprabhāsa Buddha, Ratnaketu Buddha, and Śuddharaśmiprabha Buddha as numerous as the sands of the Ganges River. Each from their own lands, has extended their vast tongues encompassing three thousand, great thousand realms, pronouncing these words of truth: 'Sentient beings, you should all believe in this discourse, The Praise of the Ineffable Virtue and Protection by All Buddhas.'

"Śāriputra, there are buddhas to the north such as Arciskandha Buddha, Vaiśvānaranirghoṣa Buddha, Duṣpradharṣa Buddha, Ādityasaṃbhava Buddha, and Jālinīprabha Buddha as numerous as the sands of the Ganges River. Each from their own lands, has extended their vast tongues encompassing three thousand, great thousand realms, pronouncing these words of truth: 'Sentient beings, you should all believe in this discourse, The Praise of the Ineffable Virtue and Protection by All Buddhas.'

"Śāriputra, there are buddhas in the lower regions such as Siṃha Buddha, Yaśas Buddha, Yaśasprabhāsa Buddha, Dharma Buddha, Dharmadhvaja Buddha, and Dharmadhara as numerous as the sands of the Ganges River. Each from their own lands, has extended their vast tongues encompassing three thousand, great thousand realms, pronouncing these words of truth: 'Sentient beings, you should all believe in this discourse, The Praise of the Ineffable Virtue and Protection by All Buddhas.'

"Śāriputra, there are buddhas in the upper regions such as Brahmaghoṣa Buddha, Nakṣatraraja Buddha, Gandhottama Buddha, Gandhaprabhāsa Buddha, Mahārciskandha Buddha, Ratnakusuma Sampuṣpitagātra Buddha, Sālendrarāja Buddha, Ratnotpalaśrī Buddha, Sarvarthadarśa Buddha, and Sumerukalpa Buddha as numerous as the sands of the Ganges River. Each from their own lands, has extended their vast tongues encompassing three thousand, great thousand realms, pronouncing these words of truth: 'Sentient beings, you should all believe in this discourse, The Praise of the Ineffable Virtue and Protection by All Buddhas.'

"Śāriputra, why do you suppose this discourse is called Protection by All Buddhas? Śāriputra should there be good men and good women who hear the buddhas' teaching of this Buddha's name, or hear the buddhas' teaching of the name of this sutra, then these good men and good women will all be protected by the all the buddhas. They will all attain the stage of non-retrogression from the path of attaining supreme perfect enlightenment. For that reason, Śāriputra, you should all believe and accept these words of mine, and the teaching of all the buddhas.

"Śāriputra, should there be people who have awakened to the aspiration, or who now awaken to the aspiration, or who will awaken to the aspiration for birth in the land of Amitāyus Buddha, then those people will all attain the stage of non-retrogression from the path of attaining supreme perfect enlightenment, and have already been born, or are now born, or will be born there. For that reason, Śāriputra, all good men and good women who believe in this should awaken to the aspiration for birth in that land.

"Śāriputra, just as I have now praised the ineffable virtue of all the buddhas, so do all the buddhas praise my ineffable virtue, ''Śākyamuni Buddha, you have accomplished this most difficult and unprecedented achievement. While being in this present world full of the five corruptions—the corruption of the age, the corruption of views, the corruption of afflictions, the corruption of human character, and the corruption of shortening lifespans—you have attained supreme perfect enlightenment, and for the sake of the sentient beings have expounded this incredible dharma that exceeds this whole mundane realm.'

"Śāriputra, you should know this. I, while being in the world of the five corruptions, have accomplished this most difficult achievement, attaining supreme perfect enlightenment, and for the sake of the whole mundane realm expounding this incredible dharma. This indeed is a difficult task."

When the Buddha finished expounding this discourse, Śāriputra and all the monks, and all the realms of celestials, mortals, asura demons, having heard the words of the Buddha, rejoiced in these words, accepted them, and believed in them. They then paid homage to the Buddha and departed.

Printed in Great Britain
by Amazon